TURNING NEGATIVE EMOTIONS INTO POSITIVE GROWTH

A PRACTICAL GUIDE TO BUILDING RESILIENCE AND EMOTIONAL WELL-BEING

RICHARD FRANCIS

Table of contents

INTRODUCTION

In the fast-paced and often challenging world we inhabit, negative emotions can seem overwhelming. These emotions—anger, sadness, fear, frustration, and others—are natural and universal. However, their intensity and frequency can sometimes hinder our personal growth, relationships, and overall well-being. Understanding and Turning Negative Emotions into Positive Growth is not merely about suppressing or ignoring them but transforming these feelings into opportunities for positive growth. This book aims to guide you on that journey.

The Ubiquity of Negative Emotions

Negative emotions are an inescapable part of the human experience. They are evolutionary responses that have helped our ancestors survive. For instance, fear can protect us from danger, while anger can motivate us to address injustices. However, in our modern lives, these emotions can often become disproportionate to the situations that trigger them, leading to unnecessary stress and conflict.

In today's society, where the pressure to succeed and the pace of life are relentless, many people find themselves struggling to cope with negative emotions. The constant barrage of information, social comparison through social media, and the demands of balancing work and personal life contribute to the prevalence of these feelings. Understanding the root causes and learning how to manage them effectively can lead to a more balanced and fulfilling life.

The Importance of Emotional Intelligence

Emotional intelligence (EI) plays a critical role in Turning Negative Emotions into Positive Growth. Emotional intelligence (EI) is the capacity to perceive, comprehend, and control one's own and others' emotions. It requires self-awareness, self-control, empathy, and social skills. High emotional intelligence can help us navigate complex social interactions, resolve conflicts, and make better decisions.

Developing emotional intelligence begins with self-awareness—recognizing and understanding our emotions and their impact on our thoughts and behaviors. This awareness allows us to identify patterns and triggers, enabling us to respond more thoughtfully rather than react impulsively. Self-regulation, another component of EI, involves managing our emotional responses, reducing the intensity and duration of negative emotions, and fostering resilience.

Empathy, the capacity to comprehend and share the emotions of others, is also important. It enhances our relationships and communication, helping us to connect more deeply and respond more compassionately. Finally, strong social skills enable us to navigate interpersonal dynamics effectively, building and maintaining healthy relationships.

The Role of Past Experiences

Our past experiences profoundly influence our emotional responses and coping mechanisms. Early childhood experiences, relationships with caregivers, and significant life events shape our beliefs and attitudes about ourselves and the world. These experiences can leave lasting imprints, creating emotional patterns that persist into adulthood.

For instance, a person who experienced consistent criticism in childhood may develop a heightened sensitivity to perceived rejection or failure. Understanding these formative experiences can provide valuable insights into our emotional triggers and patterns. By exploring and addressing the impact of the past, we can begin to heal and develop healthier ways of managing our emotions.

Therapies such as cognitive-behavioral therapy (CBT) and psychodynamic therapy can be particularly effective in uncovering and addressing these underlying issues. CBT focuses on recognizing and modifying problematic thinking patterns, while psychodynamic therapy investigates the impact of previous events on present behavior. Both approaches can help individuals gain a deeper understanding of their emotional responses and develop more adaptive coping strategies.

The Power of Mindfulness and Meditation

Mindfulness and meditation are powerful tools for Turning Negative Emotions into Positive Growth. Mindfulness involves paying attention to the present moment without judgment, cultivating awareness of our thoughts, feelings, and bodily sensations. This practice can help us become more attuned to our emotional states and reduce the tendency to react impulsively.

Meditation, a practice that often incorporates mindfulness, can further enhance emotional regulation. Regular meditation has been shown to reduce stress, anxiety, and depression, while improving attention, self-awareness, and overall emotional well-being. Techniques such as focused breathing, body scan, and loving-kindness meditation can help cultivate a sense of calm and compassion, making it easier to manage negative emotions.

Incorporating mindfulness and meditation into daily life requires consistency and practice. Even a few minutes of mindful breathing or meditation each day can make a significant difference. Over time, these practices can become a natural and integral part of our emotional self-care routine.

Developing Healthy Coping Strategies

Healthy coping strategies are essential for Turning Negative Emotions into Positive Growth effectively. These strategies can be categorized into cognitive, behavioral, and social approaches. Cognitive strategies involve changing the way we think about and interpret events, helping us to reframe negative thoughts and reduce their emotional impact.

Behavioral strategies focus on actions we can take to manage our emotions. Engaging in physical activities, such as exercise or hobbies, can provide an outlet for stress and improve mood. Relaxation techniques, such as deep breathing, progressive muscle relaxation, and visualization, can also help calm the mind and body.

Social strategies involve seeking support from others. Talking to friends, family, or a therapist can provide comfort, perspective, and practical advice. Building and maintaining strong social connections is crucial for emotional resilience, as it provides a sense of belonging and support during difficult times.

The Importance of Self-Compassion

Self-compassion is a vital component of emotional well-being. It involves treating ourselves with the same kindness, understanding, and care that we would offer to a friend. Self-compassion helps us to accept our imperfections and mistakes without harsh self-criticism, reducing the intensity of negative emotions.

Practicing self-compassion involves three main elements: self-kindness, common humanity, and mindfulness. Self-kindness means being gentle and understanding with ourselves rather than being overly critical. Recognizing our common humanity involves understanding that everyone experiences suffering and setbacks, which can help us feel less isolated in our struggles. Mindfulness enables us to monitor our thoughts and emotions without becoming overwhelmed by them.

Research has shown that self-compassion is associated with greater emotional resilience, reduced anxiety and depression, and overall psychological well-being. By cultivating self-compassion, we can develop a more balanced and compassionate relationship with ourselves, enhancing our ability to manage negative emotions.

Transforming Negativity into Positive Growth

Transforming negative emotions into positive growth involves using these experiences as opportunities for learning and self-improvement. This process requires a shift in perspective, viewing challenges and setbacks not as insurmountable obstacles, but as valuable lessons that can lead to personal growth.

Resilience is a key factor in this transformation. Resilience involves the ability to bounce back from adversity, adapt to change, and continue moving forward despite difficulties. Building resilience requires developing a positive mindset, fostering strong social connections, and practicing self-care.

Personal growth can also be facilitated by setting meaningful goals and pursuing activities that align with our values and passions. Engaging in activities that provide a sense of purpose and fulfillment can enhance our overall well-being and reduce the impact of negative emotions.

The Journey Ahead

This book is designed to be a comprehensive guide to Turning Negative Emotions into Positive Growth and transforming them into opportunities for positive growth. Each chapter will delve deeper into the topics discussed in this introduction, providing practical strategies, insights, and exercises to help you navigate your emotional landscape.

You will learn how to identify and understand your emotional triggers, develop emotional intelligence, and build healthy coping strategies. You will also explore the impact of past experiences and discover how to heal from emotional wounds. Practical tools such as mindfulness and meditation will be introduced, along with techniques for fostering self-compassion and resilience.

By the end of this journey, you will have a deeper understanding of your emotions and the skills to manage them effectively. You will be equipped to transform negative emotions into sources of strength and growth, enhancing your overall well-being and leading a more fulfilling and balanced life.

A Note on Seeking Professional Help

While this book provides a wealth of information and practical advice, it is important to recognize that Turning Negative Emotions into Positive

Growth can be a complex and challenging process. If you find that your emotions are overwhelming or significantly impacting your daily life, seeking help from a mental health professional is strongly recommended.

Therapists, counselors, and psychologists are trained to help individuals navigate their emotional challenges and develop effective coping strategies. Professional support can provide personalized guidance and support, enhancing your ability to manage negative emotions and fostering long-term emotional well-being.

Final Thoughts

Negative emotions are an inherent part of the human experience, but they do not have to dominate our lives. By understanding and managing these emotions, we can transform them into opportunities for growth and positive change. This book aims to empower you with the knowledge and tools to embark on this journey, helping you to navigate your emotional landscape with greater awareness, resilience, and compassion.

Welcome to "Turning Negative Emotions into Positive Growth: "Transforming Negativity into Positive Growth, Lasting Resilience, and Lifelong Emotional Well-Being" Let's embark on this transformative journey together, exploring the depths of our emotions and uncovering the potential for growth and fulfillment that lies within each of us.

CHAPTER 1

IDENTIFYING EMOTIONAL TRIGGERS

Identifying emotional triggers is a critical step in Turning Negative Emotions into Positive Growth effectively. Triggers are events, people, situations, or memories that provoke a strong emotional response, often disproportionate to the actual event. Understanding and identifying these triggers can help us gain control over our reactions, promote emotional resilience, and improve overall mental health.

The Importance of Identifying Emotional Triggers

Understanding what triggers our emotions is essential for several reasons:

1. Self-Awareness: Recognizing triggers enhances self-awareness. It allows us to understand the root causes of our emotional responses, providing insight into our feelings and behaviors.

2. Emotional Regulation: By identifying triggers, we can anticipate and manage our emotional responses more effectively. This proactive approach helps prevent overwhelming emotional reactions and promotes stability.

3. Relationship Management: Understanding our triggers helps improve interpersonal relationships. It allows us to communicate our needs and boundaries more clearly, reducing conflicts and fostering healthier connections.

4. Stress Reduction: Identifying and addressing triggers can significantly reduce stress levels. By mitigating the impact of triggers, we can create a more balanced and peaceful emotional state.

Common Types of Emotional Triggers

Emotional triggers can vary widely from person to person, but some common categories include:

1. External Events: Situations or occurrences in the external environment that provoke strong emotional reactions. These can include traffic jams, unexpected changes, or negative news.

2. Interpersonal Interactions: Interactions with others that elicit emotional responses. This can involve conflicts, criticism, or perceived rejection from friends, family, or colleagues.

3. Memories and Past Experiences: Memories of past events, particularly traumatic or unresolved experiences, can serve as powerful triggers. Certain sights, sounds, or smells may evoke strong emotional reactions linked to these memories.

4. Environmental Factors: Elements in the physical environment that affect emotions. This can include cluttered spaces, loud noises, or certain weather conditions.

5. Internal States: Physical or emotional states that trigger emotional responses. Hunger, fatigue, illness, or hormonal changes can all influence emotional reactivity.

Steps to Identifying Emotional Triggers

Identifying emotional triggers involves a systematic approach of self-reflection, observation, and analysis. Here are the steps to help you pinpoint your triggers:

1. Keep an Emotional Journal: Documenting your emotions and the circumstances surrounding them can provide valuable insights. Note the time, place, people involved, and your emotional reactions. Over time, patterns will emerge, highlighting common triggers.

2. Reflect on Past Experiences: Reflect on past events that elicited strong emotional responses. Consider what aspects of those events were particularly impactful. Identifying recurring themes can help pinpoint triggers.

3. Pay Attention to Physical Cues: Emotions often manifest physically. Notice any physical sensations associated with emotional reactions, such as a racing heart, tight chest, or sweating. These cues can signal that a trigger is present.

4. Identify Negative Thought Patterns: Negative thoughts often accompany emotional triggers. Pay attention to your internal dialogue when you experience strong emotions. Identifying patterns in your thoughts can help reveal underlying triggers.

5. Ask for Feedback: Sometimes, others can provide valuable perspectives on your emotional responses. Ask trusted friends, family members, or a therapist for feedback on situations where you seemed particularly reactive.

6. Practice Mindfulness: Mindfulness involves being present and fully engaged in the current moment. Practicing mindfulness can help you become more attuned to your emotions and the situations that trigger them.

Examples of Common Emotional Triggers

1. Criticism and Rejection: Many people are sensitive to criticism or rejection, which can trigger feelings of inadequacy, anger, or sadness. This may stem from past experiences of being judged or excluded.

2. Feeling Ignored or Unappreciated: Situations where you feel ignored or unappreciated can trigger emotions like frustration or resentment. This might be rooted in a need for recognition and validation.

3. Loss of Control: Events that make you feel out of control can trigger anxiety or panic. This can include unexpected changes, disruptions to routines, or situations where you feel powerless.

4. Reminders of Past Trauma: Sights, sounds, or smells associated with past trauma can serve as powerful triggers. These reminders can evoke intense emotions, including fear, sadness, or anger.

5. Perceived Threats to Relationships: Situations that threaten your relationships, such as arguments or misunderstandings, can trigger emotions like jealousy, fear, or anger. This often ties into a deep-seated fear of loss or abandonment.

6. Unmet Expectations: When reality falls short of your expectations, it can trigger disappointment, frustration, or sadness. This can apply to personal goals, relationships, or everyday situations.

Strategies for Managing Emotional Triggers

Once you've identified your emotional triggers, the next step is to develop strategies for managing them effectively. Here are some techniques to consider:

1. Cognitive Restructuring: This involves changing negative thought patterns associated with triggers. Challenge irrational beliefs and replace them with more balanced, rational thoughts.

2. Mindfulness and Grounding Techniques: Practicing mindfulness can help you stay present and reduce the impact of triggers. Grounding techniques, such as deep breathing, can also help you remain calm in triggering situations.

3. Set Boundaries: Establish clear boundaries to protect yourself from triggering situations. This might involve limiting interactions with certain people, avoiding specific environments, or communicating your needs more assertively.

4. Develop Coping Skills: Build a toolkit of coping strategies to use when you encounter triggers. This can include relaxation techniques, physical activity, creative outlets, or seeking social support.

5. Seek Professional Help: If emotional triggers are significantly impacting your life, consider seeking help from a mental health professional. Therapy can provide tailored strategies and support for managing triggers and improving emotional well-being.

6. Practice Self-Compassion: Be kind and compassionate toward yourself when you experience emotional triggers. Acknowledge your feelings without judgment and remind yourself that it's okay to have strong emotional reactions.

Understanding Personal Triggers

Understanding personal triggers is a crucial aspect of emotional self-awareness and regulation. Personal triggers are specific stimuli that provoke strong emotional reactions, often rooted in past experiences, beliefs, or unmet needs. Identifying and understanding these triggers allows individuals to manage their emotional responses better, enhance their well-being, and improve their relationships.

The Nature of Personal Triggers

Personal triggers are unique to each individual and can vary widely in their origins and manifestations. They are often linked to deeply held beliefs, past traumas, or unresolved emotional issues. When these triggers are activated, they can lead to intense emotional reactions that may seem disproportionate to the triggering event. This heightened sensitivity is a result of the underlying emotional charge associated with the trigger.

Understanding the nature of personal triggers involves exploring their sources, recognizing their impact, and learning how to manage them effectively. This process requires self-reflection, awareness, and a willingness to address underlying emotional issues.

Sources of Personal Triggers

Personal triggers can originate from various sources, including:

1. Past Experiences: Traumatic or significant events from the past can leave emotional imprints that act as triggers in the present. These experiences can include childhood traumas, relationship breakups, or significant losses.

2. Core Beliefs: Deeply held beliefs about oneself, others, and the world can influence emotional responses. For example, a belief that one is unworthy of love can trigger feelings of rejection and sadness in situations where this belief is challenged.

3. Unmet Needs: Emotional needs that were not met in the past can create sensitivities in the present. For instance, someone who did not receive enough attention or validation in childhood may be triggered by situations where they feel ignored or undervalued.

4. Cultural and Social Influences: Cultural norms and social expectations can shape emotional triggers. Societal messages about success, beauty, and behavior can create pressure and trigger feelings of inadequacy or failure.

5. Personal Values: When personal values are threatened or violated, it can trigger strong emotional reactions. For example, someone who values honesty may be deeply triggered by dishonesty or deceit.

Recognizing Personal Triggers

Recognizing personal triggers involves becoming aware of the specific situations, people, or events that consistently provoke strong emotional reactions. This process requires mindful observation and reflection on emotional patterns and responses. Here are some steps to help identify personal triggers:

1. Keep an Emotional Journal: Documenting emotional reactions and the circumstances surrounding them can reveal patterns and common triggers. Note the time, place, people involved, and your feelings.

2. Reflect on Past Experiences: Think about past events that elicited strong emotional reactions. Consider what aspects of those events were particularly impactful and how they relate to your current triggers.

3. Pay Attention to Physical Sensations: Emotions often manifest physically. Notice any physical sensations that accompany emotional reactions, such as a racing heart, tight chest, or sweating. These cues can signal the presence of a trigger.

4. Identify Negative Thought Patterns: Pay attention to your internal dialogue when you experience strong emotions. Identifying patterns in your thoughts can help reveal underlying triggers.

5. Ask for Feedback: Sometimes, others can provide valuable perspectives on your emotional responses. Ask trusted friends, family members, or a therapist for feedback on situations where you seemed particularly reactive.

6. Practice Mindfulness: Mindfulness involves being present and fully engaged in the current moment. Practicing mindfulness can help you become more attuned to your emotions and the situations that trigger them.

Understanding the Impact of Personal Triggers

Personal triggers can have significant impacts on various aspects of life, including mental health, relationships, and overall well-being. Understanding these impacts is crucial for managing triggers effectively.

1. Mental Health: Unmanaged personal triggers can contribute to mental health issues such as anxiety, depression, and chronic stress. Intense emotional reactions can create a sense of instability and overwhelm.

2. Relationships: Personal triggers can strain relationships. Emotional overreactions can lead to conflicts, misunderstandings, and emotional distance. Recognizing and addressing triggers can improve communication and foster healthier connections.

3. Physical Health: Chronic emotional stress from personal triggers can take a toll on physical health. Stress-related health issues include cardiovascular problems, weakened immune function, and digestive disorders.

4. Work and Productivity: Personal triggers can impact performance at work. Anxiety, stress, and emotional reactivity can impair concentration, decision-making, and productivity. Addressing triggers can enhance work performance and job satisfaction.

Strategies for Managing Personal Triggers

Effectively managing personal triggers requires a combination of awareness, understanding, and practical strategies. Here are some techniques to consider:

1. Cognitive Restructuring: This involves changing negative thought patterns associated with triggers. Challenge irrational beliefs and replace them with more balanced, rational thoughts.

2. Mindfulness and Grounding Techniques: Practicing mindfulness helps you stay present and observe your emotions without judgment. Grounding techniques, such as deep breathing, can help you remain calm in triggering situations.

3. Set Boundaries: Establish clear boundaries to protect yourself from triggering situations. This might involve limiting interactions with certain people, avoiding specific environments, or communicating your needs more assertively.

4. Develop Coping Skills: Build a toolkit of coping strategies to use when you encounter triggers. This can include relaxation techniques, physical activity, creative outlets, or seeking social support.

5. Seek Professional Help: If personal triggers are significantly impacting your life, consider seeking help from a mental health professional. Therapy can provide tailored strategies and support for managing triggers and improving overall well-being.

6. Practice Self-Compassion: Be kind and compassionate toward yourself when you experience emotional triggers. Acknowledge your feelings without judgment and remind yourself that it's okay to have strong emotional reactions.

Case Studies of Understanding Personal Triggers

Case Study: Emily and Social Anxiety

- Emily often felt intense anxiety in social situations, particularly at parties and large gatherings. By keeping an emotional journal, she noticed that her anxiety was triggered by fear of judgment and rejection. Reflecting on her past, Emily realized that this fear stemmed from childhood experiences of being bullied and excluded by peers.

To manage this trigger, Emily practiced cognitive restructuring, challenging her irrational beliefs about being judged. She reminded herself that most people are too focused on their own concerns to scrutinize her closely. Emily also practiced mindfulness techniques to stay present and reduce her anxiety in social situations. Over time, she became more comfortable and confident in social interactions.

Case Study: David and Workplace Stress

- David often found himself overwhelmed with anger and frustration at work, particularly during team meetings. By keeping an emotional journal, he noticed that his strong reactions were triggered by specific colleagues who he felt dismissed his ideas. Reflecting on past experiences, David realized that his sensitivity to feeling ignored stemmed from childhood experiences of not being heard by authority figures.

To manage this trigger, David practiced cognitive restructuring, reminding himself that his colleagues' reactions were not personal attacks. He also communicated his concerns more assertively, expressing his need for his ideas to be considered. By addressing his trigger and implementing practical strategies, David experienced less frustration and more productive team interactions.

The Role of Emotional Intelligence in Understanding Personal Triggers

Emotional intelligence (EI) plays a significant role in understanding and managing personal triggers. EI involves the ability to recognize, understand, and manage one's own emotions and the emotions of others. Developing emotional intelligence can enhance self-awareness, improve emotional regulation, and foster healthier relationships.

1. Self-Awareness: Self-awareness is the foundation of emotional intelligence. It involves recognizing and understanding one's emotions, including identifying personal triggers. Self-aware individuals are more attuned to their emotional responses and better equipped to manage them.

2. Self-Regulation: Self-regulation involves managing and controlling one's emotional responses. By understanding personal triggers, individuals can develop strategies to regulate their emotions effectively, reducing the impact of triggers.

3. Empathy: Empathy involves understanding and sharing the feelings of others. Developing empathy can help individuals recognize how their own triggers affect their interactions with others and foster more compassionate relationships.

4. Social Skills: Social skills involve effectively navigating social interactions and relationships. Understanding personal triggers can improve communication, reduce conflicts, and enhance interpersonal connections.

5. Motivation: Motivation involves using emotions to achieve goals and maintain a positive outlook. Understanding personal triggers can help individuals stay motivated and focused, even in challenging situations.

Developing Emotional Intelligence to Manage Personal Triggers

1. Increase Self-Awareness: Practice mindfulness and self-reflection to become more aware of your emotions and triggers. Keeping an emotional journal can also enhance self-awareness.

2. Practice Self-Regulation: Develop strategies to manage and control your emotional responses. This can include deep breathing, mindfulness meditation, and cognitive restructuring.

3. Cultivate Empathy: Practice active listening and try to understand others' perspectives. Developing empathy can improve relationships and reduce conflicts.

4. Enhance Social Skills: Work on communication and conflict-resolution skills. Understanding personal triggers can help you navigate social interactions more effectively.

5. Stay Motivated: Set realistic goals and use positive self-talk to stay motivated. Understanding personal triggers can help you overcome obstacles and maintain a positive outlook.

The Role of Therapy in Understanding Personal Triggers

Therapy can be a valuable tool for understanding and managing personal triggers. Working with a mental health professional can provide tailored strategies and support for addressing triggers and improving emotional well-being.

1. Cognitive-Behavioral Therapy (CBT): CBT is a widely used therapeutic approach that focuses on identifying and changing negative thought patterns. CBT can help individuals understand the connection between thoughts, emotions, and triggers, and develop healthier ways of thinking and responding.

2. Dialectical Behavior Therapy (DBT): DBT is a type of cognitive-behavioral therapy that emphasizes mindfulness, emotional

The Impact of Past Experiences on Turning Negative Emotions into Positive Growth

Understanding how past experiences influence our ability to manage negative emotions is crucial for personal growth and emotional resilience. Our early interactions, relationships, and significant events leave lasting imprints on our psyche, shaping our emotional responses and coping mechanisms. By examining these influences, we can gain insight into our emotional patterns and develop strategies to transform negativity into positive growth.

Emotional Imprints from Childhood

Childhood is a formative period where our emotional foundation is established. Positive early experiences, such as supportive and nurturing relationships with caregivers, foster a sense of security and self-worth. These experiences teach us how to regulate our emotions and respond to challenges constructively.

Conversely, adverse childhood experiences (ACEs), such as neglect, abuse, or the loss of a loved one, can create deep-seated emotional wounds. These negative experiences often lead to the development of maladaptive coping mechanisms. For instance, a child who faces constant criticism may grow up with a heightened sensitivity to judgment, leading to defensive or avoidant behaviors in adulthood.

Addressing the emotional imprints from childhood involves recognizing how these early experiences shape our current emotional responses. By bringing these patterns to light, we can begin to heal and develop healthier ways of Turning Negative Emotions into Positive Growth.

Formation of Core Beliefs

Core beliefs are deeply held convictions about ourselves, others, and the world, often formed in response to early life experiences. These beliefs influence our emotional responses and behavior. For example, a person who internalizes the belief that they are unworthy of love may react strongly to perceived rejection or criticism.

Negative core beliefs can perpetuate cycles of negative emotions. For instance, someone who believes they are incompetent may experience anxiety and self-doubt in challenging situations, leading to avoidance and further reinforcing their belief. Understanding the origins of these beliefs is the first step toward challenging and changing them.

Cognitive-behavioral techniques can help identify and reframe negative core beliefs. By replacing irrational and self-defeating thoughts with more balanced and positive ones, individuals can alter their emotional responses and reduce the intensity of negative emotions.

Influence on Emotional Triggers

Past experiences significantly shape our emotional triggers—specific stimuli that evoke strong emotional reactions. These triggers can be linked to unresolved traumas, unmet needs, or negative core beliefs. For instance, a person who experienced bullying may feel intense anxiety in social situations that remind them of their past.

Identifying and understanding these triggers is essential for Turning Negative Emotions into Positive Growth. Keeping an emotional journal can help track situations that provoke strong reactions, revealing patterns and underlying causes. Once identified, individuals can develop strategies to manage their responses, such as practicing mindfulness, employing grounding techniques, or seeking professional help.

Impact on Emotional Regulation

Emotional regulation refers to our ability to manage and respond to our emotions in a healthy and constructive manner. Past experiences play a crucial role in shaping our emotional regulation skills. Positive experiences, such as having supportive and responsive caregivers, teach us how to soothe ourselves and cope with stress.

In contrast, individuals who experienced neglect or inconsistent caregiving may struggle with emotional regulation. They might find it challenging to manage intense emotions, leading to outbursts, withdrawal, or other maladaptive behaviors. Understanding the roots of these difficulties can guide efforts to develop healthier emotional regulation strategies.

Therapies such as dialectical behavior therapy (DBT) can be particularly effective in enhancing emotional regulation skills. DBT teaches techniques like mindfulness, distress tolerance, and emotion regulation, which can help individuals manage their negative emotions more effectively.

Influence on Relationships

Past experiences, especially those involving significant relationships, heavily influence how we manage emotions in our current interactions. Early attachment patterns with caregivers serve as templates for future relationships. Secure attachments typically result in healthier emotional responses and better relationship management.

However, individuals with insecure attachment styles, formed through inconsistent or neglectful caregiving, may face challenges in managing emotions within relationships. For example, those with an anxious attachment style might experience heightened negative emotions in response to perceived threats to their relationships, leading to clinginess or emotional volatility.

Understanding these attachment patterns and their origins can help individuals improve their emotional responses in relationships. Couples therapy or individual therapy focusing on attachment issues can provide tools and strategies to foster healthier and more fulfilling connections.

Mental Health and Emotional Resilience

The impact of past experiences on mental health is profound, with negative experiences often contributing to the development of mental health disorders. Traumatic events, chronic stress, and adverse circumstances can lead to anxiety, depression, and other emotional difficulties.

Addressing the impact of these experiences is crucial for building emotional resilience—the ability to bounce back from adversity and manage negative emotions effectively. Therapeutic approaches such as trauma-focused therapy can help individuals process and integrate past traumas, reducing their emotional burden.

Recognizing Patterns and Recurring Themes

Recognizing patterns and recurring themes in our emotional responses is essential for Turning Negative Emotions into Positive Growth and fostering lasting resilience and emotional well-being. Our emotional reactions are often influenced by deep-seated patterns and themes that stem from past experiences, core beliefs, and habitual thought processes. By identifying and understanding these patterns, we can develop strategies to transform negativity into positive growth and improve our emotional health.

The Importance of Self-Awareness

Self-awareness is the foundation for recognizing emotional patterns and themes. It involves being mindful of our thoughts, feelings, and behaviors and understanding how they are interconnected.

Developing self-awareness allows us to observe our emotional reactions without judgment, making it easier to identify recurring patterns.

One effective way to enhance self-awareness is through regular self-reflection. Keeping a journal where you document your emotional experiences can reveal patterns over time. Note the situations that trigger strong emotions, the thoughts that accompany these feelings, and the subsequent behaviors. This practice can help you recognize consistent themes in your emotional responses.

Identifying Emotional Triggers

Emotional triggers are specific situations, people, or memories that provoke strong emotional reactions. These triggers often have roots in past experiences and can be linked to unresolved issues or unmet needs. Identifying your emotional triggers is a crucial step in recognizing patterns and recurring themes.

For example, if you notice that you frequently feel anxious in social situations, it might be due to past experiences of rejection or criticism. By understanding the underlying cause of your anxiety, you can begin to address it and develop healthier coping mechanisms.

Pay attention to your body's signals as well. Physical sensations such as a racing heart, tense muscles, or a knot in your stomach can indicate that you are experiencing an emotional trigger. Recognizing these physical cues can help you become more aware of your emotional responses and identify patterns.

Uncovering Core Beliefs

Core beliefs are deeply ingrained perceptions about ourselves, others, and the world. These beliefs are often formed in childhood and can significantly influence our emotional responses. Negative core beliefs, such as "I am not good enough" or "The world is unsafe," can lead to recurring negative emotions and behaviors.

To uncover your core beliefs, reflect on the thoughts that arise during emotional episodes. For instance, if you often feel unworthy, you might have a core belief that you are not deserving of love or success. Challenge these beliefs by examining their origins and considering evidence that contradicts them. Replacing negative core beliefs with more positive and realistic ones can help reduce the intensity of negative emotions and break recurring patterns.

Recognizing Behavioral Patterns

Our emotional patterns are closely linked to our behaviors. Recurrent behaviors, such as avoiding certain situations, reacting with anger, or seeking reassurance, can reinforce negative emotional patterns. Recognizing these behaviors and their triggers is essential for breaking the cycle of negativity.

For example, if you notice that you frequently withdraw from social interactions when feeling anxious, this behavior may be reinforcing your social anxiety. By recognizing this pattern, you can take steps to change your behavior, such as gradually exposing yourself to social situations and practicing relaxation techniques.

Behavioral patterns can also include coping mechanisms that may not be healthy in the long term, such as substance use, overeating, or procrastination. Identifying these behaviors and understanding their emotional triggers can help you develop healthier coping strategies.

Exploring Past Experiences

Past experiences play a significant role in shaping our emotional patterns and recurring themes. Traumatic events, significant losses, or chronic stress can leave lasting emotional imprints that influence our current reactions. Exploring these past experiences can provide valuable insights into our emotional patterns.

Therapeutic approaches such as cognitive-behavioral therapy (CBT) and psychodynamic therapy can help individuals explore and process past experiences. CBT focuses on identifying and changing negative thought patterns, while psychodynamic therapy delves into the influence of past experiences on current behavior. Both approaches can help individuals gain a deeper understanding of their emotional responses and develop more adaptive coping strategies.

In addition to therapy, engaging in self-reflective practices such as journaling or meditation can also facilitate the exploration of past experiences. By acknowledging and processing these experiences, you can begin to heal emotional wounds and break free from negative patterns.

The Role of Mindfulness

Mindfulness is a powerful tool for recognizing patterns and recurring themes in our emotional responses. It involves paying attention to the present moment with an open and non-judgmental attitude. Mindfulness allows us to observe our thoughts and feelings without becoming overwhelmed by them, making it easier to identify patterns.

Regular mindfulness practice can enhance self-awareness and help you recognize emotional triggers and patterns. Techniques such as mindful breathing, body scan, and mindful observation can increase your awareness of your emotional responses and provide insights into recurring themes.

By practicing mindfulness, you can create a space between your emotions and your reactions. This space allows you to respond more thoughtfully rather than reacting impulsively, reducing the intensity of negative emotions and breaking recurring patterns.

Developing New Patterns and Strategies

Once you have recognized your emotional patterns and recurring themes, the next step is to develop new patterns and strategies for managing your emotions. This involves replacing negative thought patterns with more positive and constructive ones, adopting healthier behaviors, and developing effective coping mechanisms.

1. Cognitive Restructuring: Challenge and reframe negative thoughts. Cognitive restructuring involves identifying irrational or self-defeating thoughts and replacing them with more balanced and positive ones. For example, if you have a pattern of thinking "I always fail," replace it with "I am capable of learning and improving."

2. Behavioral Changes: Modify behaviors that reinforce negative patterns. If you have a habit of avoiding situations that trigger anxiety, gradually expose yourself to these situations while practicing relaxation techniques. This can help reduce anxiety over time and break the cycle of avoidance.

3. Healthy Coping Strategies: Develop new coping mechanisms that promote emotional well-being. Engage in activities that reduce stress and improve mood, such as exercise, hobbies, or spending time with loved ones. Practice relaxation techniques such as deep breathing, progressive muscle relaxation, or visualization.

4. Seek Support: Build a support network of friends, family, or professionals who can provide encouragement and guidance. Talking to others about your experiences and emotions can provide comfort, perspective, and practical advice.

5. Practice Self-Compassion: Treat yourself with kindness and understanding. Recognize that everyone experiences negative emotions and setbacks. Practice self-compassion by acknowledging your feelings without judgment and offering yourself the same care and support that you would offer to a friend.

Embracing the Journey of Growth

Recognizing patterns and recurring themes in our emotional responses is a continuous process that requires self-awareness, patience, and commitment. It is an essential step in the journey toward Turning

Negative Emotions into Positive Growth, fostering resilience, and achieving lifelong emotional well-being.

By understanding the origins and triggers of our emotional patterns, we can develop strategies to transform negativity into positive growth. This process involves challenging negative core beliefs, modifying behaviors, and adopting healthier coping mechanisms. Through mindfulness, self-compassion, and support from others, we can break free from negative cycles and create a more fulfilling and balanced life.

CHAPTER 2

SELF-AWARENESS AND MINDFULNESS

Self-awareness and mindfulness are two fundamental practices that can profoundly impact our ability to manage negative emotions, foster resilience, and cultivate lifelong emotional well-being. These practices involve a heightened awareness of our thoughts, feelings, and behaviors, as well as a non-judgmental presence in the present moment. By integrating self-awareness and mindfulness into our daily lives, we can develop a deeper understanding of our emotional responses and learn to navigate them with greater ease and clarity.

The Concept of Self-Awareness

Self-awareness is the conscious knowledge of our own character, feelings, motives, and desires. It is the ability to introspect and recognize our internal states, which allows us to understand how our thoughts and emotions influence our actions and decisions. Self-awareness is the foundation of emotional intelligence, which encompasses the ability to manage our own emotions and understand the emotions of others.

Developing self-awareness involves several key steps:

1. Introspection: Take time to reflect on your thoughts, feelings, and behaviors. Ask yourself questions such as, "What am I feeling right now?" and "Why am I reacting this way?" This introspection helps you identify patterns and triggers in your emotional responses.

2. Emotional Monitoring: Pay attention to your emotions throughout the day. Notice how different situations, people, and thoughts affect your emotional state. This monitoring can reveal recurring themes and help you understand the root causes of your emotions.

3. Feedback from Others: Seek feedback from trusted friends, family members, or colleagues. Others can often provide insights into your behavior and emotional responses that you may not see yourself. Be open to their perspectives and use their feedback to enhance your self-awareness.

4. Self-Reflection: Engage in regular self-reflection through journaling or meditation. Writing about your experiences and emotions can help you process and understand them better. Meditation, on the other hand, allows you to observe your thoughts and feelings without judgment, fostering greater self-awareness.

The Practice of Mindfulness

Mindfulness is the practice of paying attention to the present moment with an open and non-judgmental attitude. It involves observing our thoughts, feelings, and sensations as they arise, without trying to change or suppress them. Mindfulness helps us become more attuned to our internal experiences, allowing us to respond to situations with greater clarity and calmness.

Key components of mindfulness include:

1. Present-Moment Awareness: Focus on the here and now. Instead of dwelling on the past or worrying about the future, bring your attention to the present moment. This can be achieved through practices such as mindful breathing, where you concentrate on the sensation of your breath as it enters and leaves your body.

2. Non-Judgmental Observation: Observe your thoughts and feelings without labeling them as good or bad. This non-judgmental stance allows you to accept your experiences as they are, reducing the tendency to react impulsively or negatively.

3. Body Awareness: Pay attention to the physical sensations in your body. This can help you become more aware of how your emotions manifest physically. For example, tension in your shoulders might indicate stress, while a racing heart might signal anxiety. By recognizing these bodily cues, you can address your emotions more effectively.

4. Acceptance: Embrace your thoughts and feelings without trying to change them. Acceptance does not mean resignation; rather, it means acknowledging your experiences and allowing them to be, which can reduce the struggle and resistance that often exacerbates negative emotions.

Integrating Self-Awareness and Mindfulness

Combining self-awareness and mindfulness can create a powerful synergy for Turning Negative Emotions into Positive Growth and fostering emotional well-being. Here are some practical ways to integrate these practices into your daily life:

1. Mindful Self-Reflection: Set aside time each day for mindful self-reflection. Find a quiet space, sit comfortably, and focus on your breath. As you breathe in and out, bring to mind a recent experience that triggered a strong emotional response. Observe the thoughts and feelings that arise without judgment. Reflect on what you learned about yourself from this experience and how you can apply this insight moving forward.

2. Mindful Journaling: Combine mindfulness with journaling by writing about your experiences in a mindful way. Instead of simply recounting events, focus on how you felt in each moment and what thoughts accompanied those feelings. Use this practice to explore your emotional triggers and patterns, and to gain deeper insights into your internal world.

3. Body Scan Meditation: Practice body scan meditation to enhance both self-awareness and mindfulness. Lie down or sit comfortably and bring your attention to different parts of your body, starting from your toes and moving up to your head. Notice any sensations, tension, or discomfort without trying to change them. This practice helps you connect with your body and become more aware of how emotions manifest physically.

4. Mindful Check-Ins: Throughout the day, take brief mindful check-ins. Pause for a few moments, close your eyes, and take a few deep breaths. Ask yourself, "What am I feeling right now?" and "What thoughts are running through my mind?" This practice helps you stay connected to your emotions and respond to situations with greater awareness.

5. Mindful Listening: Practice mindful listening in your interactions with others. Focus fully on the speaker, without interrupting or planning your response. Notice the emotions and thoughts that arise within you as you listen. This practice not only enhances your self-awareness but also improves your relationships by fostering empathy and understanding.

The Benefits of Self-Awareness and Mindfulness

The benefits of developing self-awareness and mindfulness are extensive and can significantly impact your emotional well-being and overall quality of life:

1. Enhanced Emotional Regulation: By becoming more aware of your emotional triggers and patterns, you can respond to situations more thoughtfully and calmly. This reduces the likelihood of impulsive reactions and helps you manage negative emotions more effectively.

2. Improved Stress Management: Mindfulness helps you stay grounded in the present moment, reducing the tendency to ruminate on past events or worry about the future. This can lower stress levels and promote a sense of calm and relaxation.

3. Greater Resilience: Self-awareness and mindfulness foster resilience by helping you understand and accept your emotions. This acceptance allows you to bounce back more quickly from setbacks and challenges, enhancing your ability to cope with adversity.

4. Better Decision-Making: Increased self-awareness allows you to recognize how your emotions influence your decisions. This awareness enables you to make more informed and balanced choices, leading to better outcomes in various aspects of life.

5. Stronger Relationships: Mindfulness and self-awareness enhance your ability to connect with others on a deeper level. By being present and attentive in your interactions, you can build stronger and more meaningful relationships.

6. Personal Growth: The insights gained from self-awareness and mindfulness can lead to significant personal growth. By understanding your strengths, weaknesses, and values, you can align your actions with your true self and pursue a more fulfilling and authentic life.

Cultivating a Lifelong Practice

Cultivating self-awareness and mindfulness is a lifelong journey that requires consistent practice and dedication. Here are some tips to help you maintain and deepen your practice over time:

1. Start Small: Begin with short, manageable practices, such as a few minutes of mindful breathing or journaling each day. Gradually increase the duration and frequency of your practice as you become more comfortable.

2. Be Patient: Developing self-awareness and mindfulness takes time and effort. Be patient with yourself and recognize that growth is a gradual process. Celebrate your progress, no matter how small, and be gentle with yourself during setbacks.

3. Seek Support: Join mindfulness or meditation groups, attend workshops, or seek guidance from a mentor or teacher. Connecting with others who share your interest in mindfulness can provide encouragement, accountability, and valuable insights.

4. Integrate Mindfulness into Daily Life: Look for opportunities to practice mindfulness throughout your day. Whether it's during your morning routine, while eating, or during your commute, find moments to bring your attention to the present and observe your thoughts and feelings.

5. Stay Open and Curious: Approach your practice with an open and curious mindset. Be willing to explore different techniques and adapt your practice to suit your needs and preferences. Stay curious about your inner world and continue to learn and grow.

The Importance of Self-Awareness and Techniques for Increasing Emotional Awareness

Self-awareness is a cornerstone of emotional intelligence, vital for personal growth, effective decision-making, and healthy relationships. It involves a deep understanding of our emotions, strengths, weaknesses, values, and triggers. Recognizing and cultivating self-awareness is essential for transforming negative emotions into positive growth, lasting resilience, and lifelong emotional well-being. Here, we delve into the importance of self-awareness and explore various techniques for increasing emotional awareness.

The Importance of Self-Awareness

1. Enhanced Emotional Regulation

Self-awareness allows us to identify and understand our emotions, which is crucial for regulating them. When we are aware of our emotional triggers and responses, we can choose how to react rather than responding impulsively. This ability to manage emotions reduces the intensity and duration of negative feelings, promoting a more balanced and calm state of mind.

2. Improved Decision-Making

Understanding our emotions helps us make better decisions. Emotions often influence our choices, and being aware of this influence allows us to approach decisions more rationally. Self-aware individuals can distinguish between emotional impulses and logical reasoning, leading to more thoughtful and effective decisions.

3. Stronger Relationships

Self-awareness enhances our ability to empathize with others and understand their perspectives. By recognizing our emotional responses, we can communicate more openly and authentically, fostering trust and connection in our relationships. Additionally, self-aware individuals are better at managing conflicts and maintaining healthy boundaries.

4. Personal Growth and Development

Self-awareness is key to personal growth. It involves recognizing our strengths and weaknesses, setting realistic goals, and striving for continuous improvement. By understanding our values and motivations, we can align our actions with our true selves, leading to a more fulfilling and purposeful life.

5. Increased Resilience

Being aware of our emotions helps us navigate challenges and setbacks more effectively. Self-aware individuals are better equipped to identify and address the root causes of their stress and anxiety. This awareness promotes resilience, enabling us to bounce back from adversity with greater ease.

6. Better Mental Health

Self-awareness contributes to better mental health by allowing us to recognize and address negative thought patterns. It enables us to identify early signs of stress, anxiety, or depression and seek appropriate help or interventions. This proactive approach to mental health fosters emotional well-being and reduces the risk of chronic psychological issues.

Techniques for Increasing Emotional Awareness

Increasing emotional awareness involves practices that help us tune into our inner experiences and understand our emotional landscape. Here are several techniques that can enhance emotional awareness:

1. Mindfulness Meditation

Mindfulness meditation involves focusing on the present moment with a non-judgmental attitude. This practice helps us observe our thoughts and emotions as they arise, fostering a deeper understanding of our internal experiences. To practice mindfulness meditation, find a quiet space, sit comfortably, and focus on your breath. Notice any thoughts, feelings, or sensations that come up without trying to change or judge them. Regular mindfulness meditation can increase emotional awareness and reduce reactivity.

2. Journaling

Keeping a journal is a powerful tool for self-reflection and emotional awareness. Writing about our experiences, thoughts, and feelings helps us process and understand them. Journaling can reveal patterns in our emotional responses and provide insights into our triggers and coping mechanisms. Set aside time each day to write about your emotions and reflect on what you have learned.

3. Body Scan Meditation

Body scan meditation involves focusing on different parts of the body and noticing any sensations without judgment. This practice helps us become more attuned to the physical manifestations of our emotions, such as tension, tightness, or relaxation. Lie down or sit comfortably, close your eyes, and slowly bring your attention to each part of your body, starting from your toes and moving up to your head. Notice any sensations and observe how they change with your breath.

4. Emotional Check-Ins

Regularly checking in with yourself throughout the day can enhance emotional awareness. Pause for a few moments, take a deep breath, and ask yourself, "What am I feeling right now?" and "What thoughts are accompanying these feelings?" This practice helps you stay connected to your emotions and recognize patterns in your emotional responses.

5. Active Listening

Active listening involves fully focusing on the speaker, understanding their message, and responding thoughtfully. By practicing active listening, we become more aware of our emotional reactions during conversations. This awareness can improve our communication skills and enhance our relationships. To practice active listening, give the speaker your full attention, avoid interrupting, and reflect back on what you have heard to ensure understanding.

6. Cognitive Behavioral Techniques

Cognitive-behavioral techniques (CBT) can help increase emotional awareness by identifying and challenging negative thought patterns. CBT involves examining the relationship between thoughts, emotions, and behaviors, and replacing irrational or harmful thoughts with more positive and realistic ones. Keeping a thought diary, where you record your thoughts, emotions, and behaviors, can help you become more aware of your cognitive patterns and their impact on your emotions.

7. Emotional Freedom Technique (EFT)

EFT, or tapping, is a practice that involves tapping on specific acupressure points on the body while focusing on a particular emotion or issue. This technique can help release negative emotions and increase emotional awareness. To practice EFT, identify an emotion or issue you want to address, tap on the acupressure points while repeating a phrase related to the emotion, and notice any changes in your emotional state.

8. Seeking Feedback

Receiving feedback from others can provide valuable insights into our emotional responses and behaviors. Ask trusted friends, family members, or colleagues for their observations about your emotional reactions and how you handle stress or conflict. Be open to their perspectives and use their feedback to enhance your self-awareness.

9. Therapy and Counseling

Working with a therapist or counselor can significantly increase emotional awareness.

Therapists can help you explore your emotions, identify patterns and triggers, and develop strategies for Turning Negative Emotions into Positive Growth. Therapy provides a safe and supportive environment for self-exploration and personal growth.

10. Practicing Gratitude

Gratitude practices can shift our focus from negative to positive emotions, increasing our overall emotional awareness. Keeping a gratitude journal, where you write down things you are grateful for each day, can help you recognize and appreciate positive experiences and emotions. This practice promotes a more balanced emotional perspective and enhances emotional well-being.

Integrating Emotional Awareness into Daily Life

Integrating emotional awareness into daily life involves consistent practice and a commitment to self-reflection. Here are some tips for maintaining and deepening your emotional awareness:

1. Create a Routine: Establish a daily routine that includes practices such as mindfulness meditation, journaling, or emotional check-ins. Consistency is key to developing and maintaining emotional awareness.

2. Be Patient and Compassionate: Developing emotional awareness takes time and effort. Be patient with yourself and recognize that growth is a gradual process. Practice self-compassion and treat yourself with kindness, especially during challenging times.

3. Stay Curious: Approach your emotions with curiosity and openness. Instead of judging or suppressing your feelings, explore them and seek to understand their origins and meanings.

4. Seek Support: Surround yourself with supportive individuals who can provide encouragement and perspective. Join groups or communities that focus on emotional well-being and mindfulness.

5. Practice Self-Care: Prioritize self-care activities that promote emotional well-being, such as exercise, healthy eating, adequate sleep, and relaxation techniques. Taking care of your physical health supports your emotional health.

CHAPTER 3

ASSESSING EMOTIONAL IMPACT

Assessing emotional impact is a pivotal process in understanding how our emotions influence our thoughts, behaviors, and overall well-being. It entails a comprehensive exploration of our emotional responses to various stimuli, enabling us to gain insights into the significance of these experiences and develop effective strategies for emotional management. By evaluating emotional impact, individuals can enhance their self-awareness, recognize patterns in their emotional reactions, and cultivate resilience in navigating life's challenges.

Understanding Emotional Impact

1. Recognition of Emotional Responses

The initial step in assessing emotional impact is acknowledging and identifying our emotional responses to different situations, events, or interactions. Emotions serve as powerful indicators of our internal reactions to external stimuli, ranging from joy and excitement to anger and sadness. By becoming attuned to how we feel in various circumstances, we lay the groundwork for understanding the emotional significance of these experiences in our lives.

2. Identification of Emotional Triggers

Emotional triggers are specific cues or stimuli that evoke strong emotional reactions within us. These triggers can be either internal (such as thoughts, memories, or beliefs) or external (such as people, places, or events). Recognizing our emotional triggers is crucial for assessing emotional impact as it allows us to pinpoint the sources of our emotional responses. This awareness empowers us to explore why certain triggers affect us deeply and develop strategies to manage our reactions constructively.

3. Evaluation of Cognitive and Behavioral Changes

Emotions have a profound influence on our cognitive processes and behavioral responses. Assessing emotional impact involves examining how our emotions shape our thoughts, beliefs, interpretations, and decision-making. For instance, feelings of fear may lead to heightened vigilance and cautious behavior, while feelings of love may promote openness and trust. By evaluating these cognitive and behavioral changes, we gain a deeper understanding of how emotions drive our actions and perceptions.

4. Awareness of Physical Manifestations

In addition to affecting our mental state, emotions manifest physically in our bodies through sensations such as muscle tension, changes in appetite, headaches, or fatigue. Assessing emotional impact requires mindfulness of these physical manifestations, as they provide valuable insights into the intensity and nature of our emotional experiences. By paying attention to these bodily cues, we can better understand the holistic impact of our emotions on our overall well-being.

5. Reflection on Emotional Patterns

Assessing emotional impact necessitates reflection on recurring emotional patterns and themes that manifest in our lives. Do certain situations consistently trigger similar emotional responses? Are there persistent emotional states or moods that influence our daily interactions and decisions? Reflecting on these patterns enables us to identify underlying causes, such as unresolved issues, core beliefs, or past experiences, that contribute to our emotional reactions.

Techniques for Assessing Emotional Impact

1. Self-Reflection and Journaling

Self-reflection and journaling serve as effective techniques for assessing emotional impact. Taking time to write about our emotional experiences, including the events that triggered specific emotions, our thoughts and beliefs at the time, and how we responded behaviorally, promotes introspection and self-awareness. Regular journaling allows us to track emotional patterns over time, identify triggers, and gain insights into our emotional resilience and growth.

2. Emotional Check-Ins

Regular emotional check-ins throughout the day foster awareness of our current emotional state and its impact on our thoughts and behaviors. Taking moments to pause, breathe deeply, and inquire about our feelings and accompanying thoughts enhances mindfulness and self-monitoring. This practice enables us to observe fluctuations in our emotional well-being and adjust our responses accordingly, promoting emotional regulation and stability.

3. Mindfulness Practices

Mindfulness practices, such as mindful breathing, body scan meditation, and mindful observation, deepen our awareness of emotional impact. These practices encourage us to observe our thoughts, emotions, and bodily sensations with acceptance and non-judgment. By cultivating mindfulness, we develop a heightened sensitivity to emotional cues and triggers, fostering resilience and adaptive coping strategies in managing challenging emotions.

4. Cognitive Behavioral Techniques (CBT)

Cognitive Behavioral Therapy (CBT) techniques are instrumental in assessing and modifying the cognitive and behavioral aspects of emotional impact. CBT involves identifying negative thought patterns, challenging irrational beliefs, and developing alternative responses to emotional triggers. Techniques such as cognitive restructuring and behavioral experiments empower individuals to reframe their interpretations of emotional experiences, cultivate self-compassion, and enhance emotional resilience.

5. Seeking Feedback and Support

Seeking feedback from trusted individuals, such as friends, family members, or mental health professionals, provides valuable perspectives on emotional impact. External feedback offers insights into how our emotions influence our interactions, relationships, and overall well-being. By engaging in open dialogue and actively listening to feedback, we gain a broader understanding of our emotional responses and opportunities for personal growth and development.

Benefits of Assessing Emotional Impact

1. Enhanced Self-Awareness

Assessing emotional impact enhances self-awareness by deepening our understanding of emotional responses, triggers, and patterns. Increased self-awareness enables us to recognize our strengths and vulnerabilities, make informed decisions, and cultivate authentic relationships. By embracing our emotional experiences with curiosity and acceptance, we foster a deeper connection with ourselves and others.

2. Improved Emotional Regulation

Understanding emotional impact facilitates effective emotional regulation and management. By identifying triggers, evaluating cognitive and behavioral responses, and practicing mindfulness and self-reflection, individuals can develop adaptive coping strategies. Enhanced emotional regulation promotes resilience in navigating stressors, enhances decision-making abilities, and fosters a balanced emotional well-being.

3. Greater Resilience and Adaptability

Assessing emotional impact cultivates resilience and adaptability in responding to life's challenges and uncertainties. By acknowledging emotional responses, reflecting on their significance, and leveraging coping techniques, individuals strengthen their capacity to bounce back from setbacks and adversity. Emotional resilience empowers individuals to embrace change, cultivate optimism, and navigate transitions with confidence and grace.

4. Enhanced Interpersonal Relationships

Awareness of emotional impact enriches interpersonal relationships by fostering empathy, communication, and mutual understanding. By recognizing and expressing emotions authentically, individuals deepen their connections with others, build trust, and resolve conflicts constructively.

Open communication and emotional authenticity contribute to healthier, more fulfilling relationships rooted in compassion and respect.

5. Personal Growth and Well-Being

Assessing emotional impact supports personal growth and well-being by promoting continuous learning, self-discovery, and fulfillment. Through self-reflection, mindfulness practices, and therapeutic interventions, individuals embark on a journey of self-improvement and transformation. Embracing emotional experiences as opportunities for growth enhances life satisfaction, promotes holistic well-being, and aligns individuals with their values and aspirations.

Short-term vs. Long-term Effects of Emotional Impact

Understanding the distinction between short-term and long-term effects of emotional impact is essential within the context of "Turning Negative Emotions into Positive Growth." It involves examining how emotions influence our immediate reactions and behaviors as well as their enduring consequences on our overall well-being and life satisfaction.

Short-term Effects of Emotional Impact

1. Immediate Emotional Responses
Short-term effects of emotional impact encompass immediate emotional responses to stimuli or events. These responses can range from intense feelings of joy or excitement to distressing emotions such as anger, fear, or sadness. The intensity and duration of these emotions vary based on individual experiences, triggers, and situational factors.

2. Behavioral Reactions
Emotional impact often manifests in short-term behavioral reactions, such as impulsive actions, avoidance behaviors, or heightened sensitivity to perceived threats. These behaviors may serve as

coping mechanisms in response to emotional distress or as expressions of emotional intensity.

3. Cognitive Processing

In the short term, emotions can influence cognitive processes such as attention, memory, and decision-making. For example, intense emotions may narrow focus on immediate threats or opportunities, affecting how information is processed and decisions are made in the moment.

4. Physiological Responses

Emotional impact is accompanied by physiological responses, including changes in heart rate, muscle tension, sweating, or gastrointestinal reactions. These bodily changes reflect the activation of the sympathetic nervous system in response to emotional arousal, preparing the body for fight-or-flight responses.

Long-term Effects of Emotional Impact

1. Emotional Residue

Long-term effects of emotional impact encompass lingering emotional residues or lasting emotional states that persist beyond the initial trigger. Unresolved emotions or recurring emotional patterns may contribute to chronic stress, mood disturbances, or emotional instability over time.

2. Cognitive Patterns and Beliefs

Emotional impact can shape long-term cognitive patterns and beliefs, influencing how individuals perceive themselves, others, and the world around them. Persistent negative emotions may contribute to cognitive distortions, self-critical thoughts, or pessimistic outlooks that impact overall mental health and well-being.

3. Behavioral Patterns and Habits

Over time, emotional impact influences behavioral patterns and habits that shape daily routines, interpersonal relationships, and life choices. Chronic emotional distress may lead to maladaptive coping strategies, substance use, or avoidance behaviors that perpetuate negative cycles and hinder personal growth.

4. Physical Health

Long-term emotional impact can affect physical health through prolonged exposure to stress hormones, immune system suppression, or increased risk of cardiovascular disease. Chronic emotional distress may contribute to inflammation, sleep disturbances, or other physical health conditions that impact overall quality of life.

Balancing Short-term and Long-term Effects

Turning Negative Emotions into Positive Growth within the framework of "Turning Negative Emotions into Positive Growth" involves balancing short-term and long-term effects to promote emotional resilience and well-being. Strategies include:

Mindful Awareness: Cultivating mindfulness to observe short-term emotional responses without immediate reaction, fostering greater self-regulation and emotional stability.

Cognitive Restructuring: Challenging negative cognitive patterns and beliefs to promote long-term emotional resilience and adaptive coping strategies.

Behavioral Modification: Implementing positive behavioral changes and habits that support emotional well-being and reduce the impact of chronic emotional distress.

Seeking Support: Engaging in supportive relationships, therapy, or community resources to address both short-term emotional reactions and long-term emotional challenges effectively.

The Ripple Effect of Emotional Impact on Relationships and Work

Emotions, both positive and negative, wield a profound influence over various aspects of our lives, including our relationships and professional environments. By recognizing how our emotional states affect interactions and performance, we can develop strategies to foster healthier relationships and more productive work environments.

The Ripple Effect on Relationships

1. Emotional Contagion

Emotions are contagious; they can spread from one person to another, influencing the mood and behavior of those around us. When we experience negative emotions, such as anger, frustration, or sadness, these feelings can affect our interactions with others. Emotional contagion can lead to a cycle where negativity is perpetuated within relationships, causing strain and misunderstandings.

2. Communication and Conflict

Emotional impact significantly influences communication patterns within relationships. When negative emotions dominate, communication can become strained, leading to misunderstandings and conflicts. Anger, for example, can cause individuals to speak harshly or become defensive, making it difficult to resolve disagreements constructively.

Effective communication requires emotional awareness and regulation. By Turning Negative Emotions into Positive Growth, individuals can engage in more open, honest, and empathetic conversations. This approach not only prevents conflicts but also strengthens the bond between individuals, promoting trust and mutual respect.

3. Empathy and Understanding

Empathy is the ability to understand and share the feelings of others. Negative emotions, particularly those rooted in personal insecurities or stress, can hinder our capacity for empathy. When we are preoccupied with our own emotional turmoil, we may struggle to connect with others' experiences and provide the support they need.

Cultivating empathy requires managing our own emotional states. By addressing and transforming negative emotions, we can become more attuned to the feelings of others. This enhances our ability to offer compassion and understanding, creating deeper and more meaningful connections in our relationships.

4. Trust and Intimacy

Trust is the foundation of any healthy relationship. Negative emotions, especially those linked to past betrayals or disappointments, can erode trust and intimacy. When individuals carry unresolved negative emotions into their relationships, they may become guarded or suspicious, preventing the development of genuine closeness.

Turning Negative Emotions into Positive Growth involves processing past hurts and letting go of emotional baggage. By doing so, individuals can approach relationships with an open heart, fostering trust and intimacy. This not only strengthens the relationship but also enhances overall emotional well-being.

5. Support and Resilience

Positive relationships provide essential support systems during challenging times. When negative emotions are managed effectively, individuals are more likely to seek and offer support within their relationships. This mutual support builds resilience, helping individuals navigate life's ups and downs with greater ease.

The Ripple Effect on Work

1. Performance and Productivity

Emotional impact extends to the workplace, influencing performance and productivity. Negative emotions such as stress, anxiety, and frustration can impair cognitive functions, leading to decreased focus, creativity, and efficiency. Employees who are overwhelmed by negative emotions may struggle to meet deadlines, complete tasks, or contribute effectively to team projects.

By Turning Negative Emotions into Positive Growth, individuals can enhance their work performance. Techniques such as mindfulness, cognitive restructuring, and stress management can reduce the impact of negative emotions, allowing employees to maintain clarity and productivity even in challenging situations.

2. Decision-Making and Problem-Solving

Emotions play a crucial role in decision-making and problem-solving processes. Negative emotions, particularly those driven by fear or anger, can cloud judgment and lead to impulsive or irrational decisions. For example, a manager under stress may make hasty decisions without considering all relevant factors, potentially causing negative consequences for the team or organization.

Effective emotional management supports better decision-making by promoting a balanced and thoughtful approach. By recognizing and addressing negative emotions, individuals can approach problems with a clear mind, consider multiple perspectives, and make informed decisions that benefit both themselves and their workplace.

3. Workplace Relationships and Collaboration

The ripple effect of emotional impact is evident in workplace relationships and collaboration. Negative emotions can create tension and conflict among colleagues, hindering teamwork and cooperation. For instance, an employee who feels undervalued or stressed may become withdrawn or confrontational, affecting team dynamics and overall morale.

Fostering a positive emotional environment at work involves managing personal emotions and contributing to a supportive culture. Encouraging open communication, empathy, and mutual respect can mitigate the negative impact of emotions and promote effective collaboration. When employees feel emotionally supported, they are more likely to engage in productive teamwork and contribute positively to the organizational goals.

4. Leadership and Management

Leaders and managers have a significant influence on the emotional climate of the workplace. Their emotional states and responses set the tone for the team or organization. Negative emotions in leaders, such as frustration or impatience, can trickle down to employees, creating a stressful and demotivating work environment.

Effective leaders recognize the importance of managing their emotions to inspire and motivate their teams. By demonstrating emotional resilience and positive coping strategies, leaders can create a culture of trust, support, and innovation. This approach not only enhances employee satisfaction and retention but also drives organizational success.

5. Work-Life Balance and Well-Being

Emotional impact extends beyond the workplace, affecting work-life balance and overall well-being. Negative emotions at work can spill over into personal life, causing stress and affecting relationships outside of work. Similarly, unresolved negative emotions from personal life can impact work performance and interactions with colleagues.

Maintaining a healthy work-life balance requires effective emotional management. Techniques such as setting boundaries, practicing self-care, and seeking support can help individuals navigate the demands of work and personal life. By addressing negative emotions proactively, individuals can achieve a more harmonious balance, enhancing their overall quality of life.

Strategies for Managing Emotional Impact

1. Mindfulness and Emotional Awareness

Mindfulness practices enhance emotional awareness, allowing individuals to observe their emotions without immediate reaction. By cultivating mindfulness, individuals can identify emotional triggers, recognize patterns, and develop healthier responses. This approach is particularly effective in managing the ripple effect of emotions in both relationships and work.

2. Cognitive Behavioral Techniques

Cognitive Behavioral Therapy (CBT) techniques are valuable tools for Turning Negative Emotions into Positive Growth. These techniques involve identifying and challenging negative thought patterns, reframing irrational beliefs, and developing alternative responses. By applying CBT principles, individuals can reduce the impact of negative emotions on their relationships and work performance.

3. Communication and Conflict Resolution

Effective communication is key to managing the emotional impact on relationships and work. Developing active listening skills, practicing empathy, and engaging in constructive conflict resolution can mitigate the negative effects of emotions. By fostering open and honest communication, individuals can build stronger connections and resolve conflicts amicably.

4. Stress Management and Self-Care

Managing stress is essential for mitigating the ripple effect of negative emotions. Techniques such as exercise, relaxation, and hobbies can reduce stress and promote emotional well-being. Prioritizing self-care ensures that individuals have the emotional resources to navigate challenges in both personal and professional domains.

5. Seeking Support and Professional Help

Seeking support from trusted individuals or professionals can provide valuable insights and strategies for Turning Negative Emotions into Positive Growth. Therapy, coaching, or support groups offer a safe space to explore emotions, gain perspective, and develop effective coping mechanisms. By seeking help, individuals can enhance their emotional resilience and overall well-being.

CHAPTER 4

CHALLENGING NEGATIVE THOUGHTS

Negative thoughts can significantly impact our emotional well-being, relationships, and overall quality of life. challenging negative thoughts is a crucial step in transforming negativity into positivity. This chapter explores various techniques and strategies to identify, challenge, and reframe negative thoughts, fostering a healthier mindset and emotional resilience.

Understanding Negative Thoughts

1. The Nature of Negative Thoughts

Negative thoughts are cognitive distortions or irrational beliefs that often arise in response to stress, anxiety, or challenging situations. These thoughts can be automatic, persistent, and intrusive, leading to a cycle of negativity that affects emotions, behavior, and overall mental health.

Common types of negative thoughts include:
- **Catastrophizing:** Exaggerating the potential negative outcomes of a situation.
- **Overgeneralization:** Drawing broad, negative conclusions based on a single event.
- **Black-and-White Thinking:** Viewing situations in extremes, with no middle ground.
- **Personalization:** Blaming oneself for events beyond one's control.
- **Mind Reading:** Assuming others are thinking negatively about oneself.

2. The Impact of Negative Thoughts

Negative thoughts can have a profound impact on various aspects of life, including:

- **Emotional Well-Being:** Persistent negative thoughts contribute to feelings of sadness, anxiety, and hopelessness.
- **Behavior:** Negative thinking patterns can lead to avoidance, procrastination, and other maladaptive behaviors.
- **Relationships:** Negative thoughts can strain relationships by fostering misunderstandings, conflicts, and a lack of trust.
- **Physical Health:** Chronic negativity can increase stress levels, leading to physical symptoms such as headaches, fatigue, and weakened immunity.

Identifying Negative Thoughts

1. Increasing Self-Awareness

The first step in challenging negative thoughts is to become aware of them. This involves paying attention to one's internal dialogue and recognizing patterns of negativity. Techniques to increase self-awareness include:

- **Mindfulness Meditation:** Practicing mindfulness helps individuals observe their thoughts without judgment, fostering greater awareness of negative thinking patterns.
- **Journaling:** Writing down thoughts and feelings can help identify recurring negative thoughts and triggers.
- **Emotional Check-Ins:** Regularly assessing one's emotional state and identifying the thoughts associated with negative emotions can increase self-awareness.

2. Cognitive Behavioral Techniques

Cognitive Behavioral Therapy (CBT) offers practical tools for identifying negative thoughts. These techniques involve:

- **Thought Records:** Keeping a log of negative thoughts, the situations that triggered them, and the associated emotions can help individuals recognize patterns and triggers.

- **Cognitive Restructuring:** Examining and challenging the validity of negative thoughts to identify cognitive distortions.

Challenging Negative Thoughts

1. Examining the Evidence

One effective strategy for challenging negative thoughts is to examine the evidence for and against them. This involves:

- **Questioning Assumptions:** Asking oneself whether there is factual evidence to support the negative thought or if it is based on assumptions or interpretations.
- **Seeking Alternative Explanations:** Considering other possible explanations for a situation can help shift perspectives and reduce negativity.
- **Testing Predictions:** Evaluating past experiences to see if negative predictions have come true can provide a more balanced view of future outcomes.

For example, if someone thinks, "I always fail at everything," they can challenge this thought by examining instances where they succeeded and acknowledging that failure is not a constant outcome.

2. Reframing Negative Thoughts

Reframing involves changing the way one interprets a situation to create a more balanced and positive perspective. Techniques for reframing include:

- **Positive Reinterpretation:** Finding the silver lining or positive aspect of a challenging situation.
- **Perspective Taking:** Considering how someone else might view the situation can provide new insights and reduce negativity.
- **Future Focus:** Shifting focus from past mistakes or current difficulties to future possibilities and opportunities.

For instance, instead of thinking, "I'm terrible at this job," one can reframe the thought to, "I'm still learning and improving, and I have the potential to get better."

3. Practicing Self-Compassion

Self-compassion involves treating oneself with kindness and understanding during difficult times, rather than being self-critical. This approach helps counteract negative thoughts by fostering a supportive and nurturing inner dialogue. Strategies for practicing self-compassion include:

- **Self-Kindness:** Speaking to oneself with the same kindness and encouragement that one would offer to a friend.
- **Common Humanity:** Recognizing that everyone makes mistakes and experiences difficulties, which helps reduce feelings of isolation.
- **Mindfulness:** Observing negative thoughts and emotions without judgment and accepting them as part of the human experience.

By practicing self-compassion, individuals can challenge harsh self-criticism and replace it with a more balanced and supportive perspective.

Cognitive Behavioral Techniques for Challenging Negative Thoughts

1. Socratic Questioning

Socratic questioning is a technique used in CBT to challenge negative thoughts by asking probing questions. This method encourages individuals to critically examine their thoughts and consider alternative viewpoints. Key questions include:

- What evidence supports this thought?
- Is there an alternative explanation?
- What is the worst that could happen, and how likely is it?
- What is the best that could happen?
- How would I advise a friend in this situation?

By answering these questions, individuals can gain a more balanced perspective and reduce the impact of negative thoughts.

2. Behavioral Experiments

Behavioral experiments involve testing the validity of negative thoughts through real-life experiences. This technique helps individuals gather evidence that challenges their negative beliefs. Steps for conducting a behavioral experiment include:

- Identifying a Negative Thought: Choose a specific negative thought to test.
- Formulating a Hypothesis: Develop a prediction based on the negative thought.
- Planning an Experiment: Design an activity or situation to test the hypothesis.
- Recording Results: Document the outcomes of the experiment.
- Reflecting on Findings: Compare the

results with the original prediction and consider how they challenge the negative thought.

For example, if someone believes, "People will judge me if I speak up in meetings," they can conduct a behavioral experiment by actively participating in a meeting and observing the reactions of others.

3. Thought Stopping

Thought stopping is a technique used to interrupt and change the flow of negative thoughts. It involves:
- Awareness: Recognizing when a negative thought occurs.
  - **Interruption:** Using a physical or mental cue (such as saying "stop" or visualizing a stop sign) to interrupt the thought.
  - **Replacement:** Shifting focus to a positive or neutral thought or engaging in a distracting activity.

Thought stopping can help individuals break the cycle of negativity and redirect their attention to more constructive thoughts and activities.

4. Affirmations and Positive Self-Talk

Affirmations are positive statements that individuals repeat to themselves to counteract negative thoughts and build self-confidence. Effective affirmations are:

- **Positive:** Focused on what one wants to achieve or believe.
- **Present Tense:** Framed as if they are already true.
- **Personal:** Reflecting individual values and goals.

Examples of affirmations include:
- "I am capable and confident in my abilities."
- "I deserve happiness and success."
- "I am resilient and can handle challenges with grace."

Positive self-talk involves replacing negative thoughts with encouraging and supportive statements. By practicing affirmations and positive self-talk, individuals can rewire their thinking patterns and foster a more optimistic outlook.

Integrating Techniques into Daily Life

1. Developing a Routine

Integrating techniques for challenging negative thoughts into daily life requires consistency and practice. Developing a routine that includes mindfulness, journaling, and cognitive restructuring can help reinforce positive thinking patterns. For example:

- **Morning Routine:** Begin the day with mindfulness meditation or positive affirmations.
- **Daily Journaling:** Reflect on thoughts and emotions in a journal, identifying and challenging negative thoughts.
- **Evening Reflection:** Review the day's experiences, focusing on positive achievements and growth.

2. Building a Support System

Having a support system is essential for maintaining emotional well-being and challenging negative thoughts. Friends, family, and mental health professionals can provide valuable feedback, encouragement, and perspective. Building a support system involves:

- **Open Communication:** Sharing thoughts and feelings with trusted individuals.
- **Seeking Feedback:** Asking for constructive feedback and alternative viewpoints.
- **Professional Support:** Engaging in therapy or counseling to explore and challenge negative thoughts with the guidance of a trained professional.

3. Practicing Self-Care

Self-care is a vital component of emotional well-being and resilience. Regular self-care practices can reduce stress and create a positive foundation for challenging negative thoughts. Self-care activities include:

- **Physical Exercise:** Engaging in regular physical activity to boost mood and reduce stress.
- **Healthy Nutrition:** Eating a balanced diet to support physical and mental health.
- **Relaxation Techniques:** Practicing relaxation methods such as deep breathing, yoga, or progressive muscle relaxation.
- **Hobbies and Interests:** Participating in activities that bring joy and fulfillment.

1. Visualization Techniques

Visualization involves mentally rehearsing positive outcomes or imagining a calming scene to counteract negative thoughts. Techniques include:

- **Positive Outcome Visualization:** Imagine successfully navigating a challenging situation and focus on the positive feelings associated with that success.

- **Calm Scene Visualization:** Picture a serene environment, such as a beach or forest, to induce relaxation and interrupt negative thought patterns.

Visualization can be particularly effective before stressful events, helping to reduce anxiety and build confidence.

2. Exposure Therapy

Exposure therapy is a technique often used to address fears and phobias, but it can also be applied to challenge negative thoughts. This involves gradually facing feared situations or thoughts in a controlled and systematic way. Steps include:

- **Identify Triggers:** Determine specific situations or thoughts that cause distress.
- **Develop a Hierarchy:** Rank these triggers from least to most anxiety-provoking.
- **Gradual Exposure:** Begin with the least distressing trigger and gradually work up the

hierarchy, using relaxation techniques to manage anxiety during exposure.

Exposure therapy helps to reduce avoidance behaviors and demonstrate that feared outcomes are often less catastrophic than anticipated.

3. Problem-Solving Skills

Improving problem-solving skills can empower individuals to tackle challenges directly, reducing feelings of helplessness associated with negative thoughts. Problem-solving steps include:

- **Define the Problem:** Clearly identify the issue causing distress.
- **Generate Solutions:** Brainstorm possible solutions without evaluating them initially.
- **Evaluate Options:** Assess the pros and cons of each potential solution.

- **Choose and Implement:** Select the best option and take actionable steps to implement it.
- **Review and Adjust:** Evaluate the outcome and make adjustments as necessary.

Effective problem-solving enhances confidence and reduces the frequency of negative thoughts by providing practical ways to address challenges.

4. Gratitude Practice

Focusing on gratitude can shift attention away from negative thoughts and foster a more positive outlook. Techniques include:

- **Gratitude Journaling:** Regularly write down things you are grateful for, focusing on specific details.
- **Gratitude Letters:** Write letters expressing appreciation to people who have positively impacted your life.
- **Gratitude Meditation:** Practice mindfulness meditation centered on feelings of gratitude.

By cultivating gratitude, individuals can counteract negative thoughts and increase overall emotional well-being.

5. Acceptance and Commitment Therapy (ACT)

ACT involves accepting negative thoughts and emotions rather than trying to eliminate them. The focus is on committing to actions that align with one's values. Key components include:

- **Acceptance:** Allow negative thoughts and feelings to exist without trying to change them.
- **Cognitive Defusion:** Separate oneself from thoughts by observing them without attachment.
- **Values Clarification:** Identify core values and commit to actions that reflect these values.

- **Mindfulness:** Practice staying present and engaged in the current moment.

ACT helps individuals focus on meaningful actions rather than becoming entangled in negative thoughts.

Integrating Techniques into Daily Life

1. Creating a Supportive Environment

A supportive environment can reinforce positive thinking and emotional well-being. Strategies include:

Positive Surroundings: Surround yourself with positive influences, such as inspirational books, uplifting music, and encouraging people.

Declutter: Reduce physical clutter to create a calm and organized space, which can help clear mental clutter as well.

Positive Reminders: Use visual reminders, such as sticky notes with affirmations, to reinforce positive thoughts throughout the day.

2. Regular Reflection

Regular reflection on progress and challenges can help maintain a positive trajectory. Techniques include:

Weekly Reviews: Set aside time each week to reflect on successes, identify areas for improvement, and adjust strategies as needed.

Accountability Partners: Partner with someone who can provide support, encouragement, and feedback on your progress.

3. Continuous Learning

Continual learning and growth are essential for long-term emotional well-being. Engage in activities that promote personal development, such as:

Reading: Explore books and articles on emotional intelligence, positive psychology, and personal growth.

Workshops and Seminars: Attend events that offer new insights and skills for managing negative thoughts.

Online Courses: Enroll in courses that focus on cognitive behavioral techniques, mindfulness, and other relevant topics.

By committing to continuous learning, individuals can stay motivated and equipped with new tools to challenge negative thoughts effectively.

4. Balancing Activities

Balancing work, leisure, and rest is crucial for maintaining emotional resilience. Strategies include:

Time Management: Plan and prioritize activities to ensure a healthy balance between work and personal life.

Leisure Activities: Engage in hobbies and activities that bring joy and relaxation.

Rest and Recovery: Ensure adequate rest and downtime to recharge and prevent burnout.

Maintaining a balanced lifestyle supports overall well-being and enhances the ability to manage negative thoughts.

5. Celebrating Successes

Acknowledging and celebrating successes, no matter how small, can reinforce positive thinking and build confidence. Techniques include:

Progress Tracking:Keep a journal or chart to track progress and milestones.

Reward System: Set up a reward system to celebrate achievements, such as treating yourself to something enjoyable.

Share Successes: Share accomplishments with supportive friends or family members to reinforce positive reinforcement.

Reframing Negative Situations

Reframing is a cognitive-behavioral technique that involves changing the way we perceive and interpret negative situations. By altering our perspective, we can transform our emotional responses and reactions, leading to a more positive outlook and greater resilience.Reframing doesn't mean denying or ignoring the challenges we face. Instead, it involves acknowledging the difficulties while consciously choosing to see them from a different angle. This shift in perspective can reveal new possibilities, opportunities for growth, and a deeper understanding of our experiences.

The Power of Perception

Our perception of events significantly influences our emotional responses. Two people can experience the same event but have completely different reactions based on how they interpret it. For example, being stuck in traffic might be seen by one person as an opportunity to listen to a favorite podcast, while another person might view it as a source of frustration and stress. The event itself is neutral; it's our interpretation that gives it meaning.

Understanding the power of perception allows us to take control of our emotional responses. By consciously choosing to reframe negative situations, we can reduce stress, enhance our problem-solving abilities, and improve our overall well-being.

Techniques for Reframing Negative Situations

1. Identify the Negative Thought

The first step in reframing is to become aware of the negative thought or belief. This requires self-awareness and mindfulness, as negative thoughts can often be automatic and go unnoticed. Once we identify the thought, we can begin to challenge and reframe it.

Example:
- **Negative Thought:** "I always mess up in important meetings."

- **Identified Thought:** Recognizing that this thought arises before or during significant work presentations.

2. Examine the Evidence

Next, evaluate the evidence for and against the negative thought. This involves questioning the validity of the thought and considering alternative explanations.

Example:
- **Evidence Against:** Recall instances where meetings went well or where mistakes were minor and had no significant impact.
- **Alternative Explanations:** Recognize that everyone makes mistakes occasionally, and one mistake does not define overall competence.

3. Challenge the Thought

Ask yourself if the thought is based on facts or assumptions. Are there cognitive distortions at play, such as overgeneralization or catastrophizing? Challenging these distortions can help break the cycle of negative thinking.

Example:

- **Challenging Overgeneralization:** Remind yourself that making a mistake in one meeting does not mean you always mess up.

4. Reframe the Thought

Create a more balanced and constructive perspective. This involves turning the negative thought into a positive or neutral one.

Example:

- **Reframed Thought:** "I've had successful meetings before, and I can learn from any mistakes to improve in the future."

5. Focus on Learning and Growth

Emphasize what can be learned from the situation. Negative experiences often provide valuable lessons that contribute to personal and professional growth.

Example:

- **Learning Perspective:** "This mistake is an opportunity to refine my presentation skills and prepare better next time."

6. Use Positive Affirmations

Incorporate positive affirmations to reinforce the reframed perspective. Affirmations help shift focus away from negativity and build self-confidence.

Example:

- **Affirmation:** "I am capable and prepared. I can handle challenges and learn from every experience."

Practical Applications of Reframing

Reframing can be applied to various aspects of life, including work, relationships, and personal challenges. Here are some practical examples:

1. Work-Related Challenges

Scenario:
- **Situation:** You didn't get a promotion you were hoping for.
- **Negative Thought:** "I'm not good enough for this job."

Reframing:
- **Examine Evidence:** Consider positive feedback from colleagues and past achievements.
- **Alternative Explanation:** The decision might have been influenced by factors beyond your control, such as company politics or budget constraints.
- **Reframe:** "While I didn't get the promotion this time, I can seek feedback to improve and pursue future opportunities."

2. Relationship Conflicts

Scenario:

- **Situation:** An argument with a friend leaves you feeling hurt and misunderstood.
- **Negative Thought:** "They don't care about me."

Reframing:

- **Examine Evidence:** Reflect on past positive interactions and support from the friend.
- **Alternative Explanation:** The friend might be dealing with their own stress or issues, which affected their behavior.
- **Reframe:** "This conflict doesn't define our friendship. I can communicate my feelings and work towards understanding and resolution."

3. Personal Setbacks

Scenario:

- **Situation:** A health goal, such as losing weight, isn't progressing as quickly as hoped.
- **Negative Thought:** "I'm a failure and will never reach my goals."

Reframing:

- **Examine Evidence:** Acknowledge small progress and positive changes in habits.
- **Alternative Explanation:** Progress takes time, and setbacks are a normal part of any journey.
- **Reframe:** "I've made some progress and learned more about what works for me. I can adjust my plan and keep moving forward."

Building a Habit of Reframing

Like any skill, reframing takes practice and consistency. Here are some tips to build a habit of reframing negative situations:

1. Practice Daily

Incorporate reframing into your daily routine. Start with small, everyday situations and gradually apply the technique to more significant challenges.

2. Use a Journal

Keep a journal to document negative thoughts and your efforts to reframe them. Reflect on the progress and patterns over time.

3. Seek Support

Share your reframing efforts with a trusted friend, family member, or therapist. They can provide additional perspectives and encouragement.

4. Be Patient

Change takes time, and it's normal to revert to old thinking patterns occasionally. Be patient with yourself and celebrate small victories along the way.

5. Stay Mindful

Mindfulness practices, such as meditation and deep breathing, can enhance self-awareness and make it easier to catch and reframe negative thoughts.

CHAPTER 5

MINDFULNESS AND MEDITATION PRACTICES

Mindfulness is the practice of paying attention to the present moment without judgment. It involves being fully aware of our thoughts, emotions, bodily sensations, and the environment around us. By cultivating mindfulness, we can develop a deeper understanding of our inner experiences and respond to them with greater clarity and composure.

Mindfulness is rooted in ancient Buddhist traditions but has been widely adopted in modern psychology and wellness practices due to its proven benefits for mental health and emotional well-being. When we practice mindfulness, we create a space to observe our thoughts and feelings without getting caught up in them, allowing us to manage negative emotions more effectively.

The Benefits of Mindfulness

1. Reduced Stress: Mindfulness helps to reduce stress by promoting relaxation and encouraging a non-reactive approach to stressors.

2. Improved Emotional Regulation: By becoming more aware of our emotions, we can respond to them in healthier ways rather than reacting impulsively.

3. Enhanced Focus and Concentration: Mindfulness practices can improve attention and cognitive functioning, making it easier to stay focused on tasks.

4. Greater Self-Awareness: Mindfulness fosters a deeper understanding of our thoughts, feelings, and behaviors, leading to increased self-awareness and personal growth.

5. Better Relationships: Mindfulness enhances empathy and communication, improving our interactions and relationships with others.

Introduction to Meditation

Meditation is a core practice within mindfulness, involving focused attention and awareness to achieve a mentally clear and emotionally calm state. There are various types of meditation, each with its unique approach, but they all share the common goal of quieting the mind and fostering inner peace.

Types of Meditation Practices

1. Focused Attention Meditation:
- **Technique:** Focus your attention on a single object, such as your breath, a mantra, or a candle flame. Whenever your mind wanders, gently bring your focus back to the chosen object.

- **Benefits:** Enhances concentration and mindfulness by training the mind to stay present.

2. Body Scan Meditation:
- **Technique:** Lie down or sit comfortably. Bring your attention to different parts of your body, starting from your toes and moving up to your head. Notice any sensations, tension, or areas of relaxation.
- **Benefits:** Promotes body awareness and relaxation, reducing physical and mental tension.

3. Loving-Kindness Meditation (Metta):
- **Technique:** Begin by generating feelings of love and kindness towards yourself. Gradually extend these feelings to loved ones, acquaintances, and even those you have conflicts with. Finally, extend the feelings to all beings.
- **Benefits:** Enhances empathy, compassion, and emotional well-being.

4. Mindfulness Meditation:

- **Technique:** Sit comfortably and focus on your breath or bodily sensations. Allow thoughts and feelings to arise without judgment, observing them as they come and go.
- **Benefits:** Cultivates present-moment awareness and reduces reactivity to thoughts and emotions.

5. Transcendental Meditation (TM):

- **Technique:** Practice involves silently repeating a specific mantra for 20 minutes twice a day while sitting comfortably.
- **Benefits:** Promotes deep relaxation and reduces stress.

Incorporating Mindfulness and Meditation into Daily Life

1. Daily Practice:

- Set aside a specific time each day for mindfulness and meditation practice. Consistency is key to reaping the benefits.
- Start with short sessions (5-10 minutes) and gradually increase the duration as you become more comfortable.

2. Mindful Breathing:

- Practice mindful breathing throughout the day by taking a few moments to focus on your breath. Inhale deeply through your nose, hold for a few seconds, and exhale slowly through your mouth.
- Use this technique during stressful situations to center yourself and calm your mind.

3. Mindful Walking:

- Turn your daily walk into a mindfulness practice by paying attention to each step, the sensation of your feet touching the ground, and the environment around you.
- Walk slowly and deliberately, noticing the sights, sounds, and smells.

4. Mindful Eating:

- Engage in mindful eating by savoring each bite of food. Pay attention to the taste, texture, and aroma.
- Eat slowly and without distractions, appreciating the nourishment provided by your meal.

5. Mindful Listening:

- Practice mindful listening in your conversations. Give your full attention to the speaker without interrupting or planning your response.
- Focus on their words, tone, and body language, fostering better communication and connection.

Guided Meditation and Resources

1. Guided Meditations:

- Utilize guided meditation recordings or apps to help you stay focused and engaged during your practice. These resources provide instructions and support for various types of meditation.

2. Mindfulness Apps:

- Apps like Headspace, Calm, and Insight Timer offer a wide range of mindfulness and meditation practices, including guided sessions, sleep aids, and stress-relief techniques.

Overcoming Challenges in Meditation

1. Restlessness and Distraction:

- It's normal to feel restless or distracted during meditation. When this happens, gently bring your focus back to your breath or chosen object without judgment.

2. Impatience:

- Progress in meditation can be slow and subtle. Practice patience and persistence, recognizing that benefits accumulate over time.

3. Self-Judgment:

- Avoid judging your meditation practice. There is no "right" way to meditate. Each session is a learning experience, regardless of how focused or distracted you feel.

4. Physical Discomfort:

- Find a comfortable posture that allows you to stay alert and relaxed. Use cushions or chairs if needed to support your body.

The Role of Mindfulness in Turning Negative Emotions into Positive Growth

1. Enhanced Emotional Awareness:

- Mindfulness increases our awareness of emotions as they arise, allowing us to recognize and acknowledge them without being overwhelmed.

2. Non-Reactivity:

- By observing emotions without judgment, we can respond to them more thoughtfully rather than reacting impulsively.

3. Acceptance:
- Mindfulness encourages acceptance of all emotions, including negative ones, as natural and transient experiences. This acceptance reduces resistance and emotional suffering.

4. Empowerment:
- Through mindfulness, we gain a sense of control over our emotional responses. We learn that while we cannot always change external circumstances, we can choose how we respond to them.

Integrating Mindfulness into Daily Life

Mindfulness is more than just a practice; it's a way of life that can be seamlessly integrated into everyday activities. By incorporating mindfulness into our daily routines, we can enhance our overall well-being, reduce stress, and manage negative emotions more effectively. integrating mindfulness into daily life is a crucial step towards achieving lasting emotional health.

The Importance of Consistent Practice

Consistency is key when it comes to mindfulness. While occasional meditation sessions can be beneficial, the true power of mindfulness is unlocked when it becomes a regular part of our daily routine. This doesn't necessarily mean setting aside large chunks of time each day; even brief moments of mindfulness can make a significant difference.

Practical Strategies for Daily Mindfulness

1. Mindful Morning Routine

Starting the day with mindfulness can set a positive tone and help you approach the day with greater calm and clarity. Consider the following practices:

- **Morning Meditation:** Spend a few minutes in meditation as soon as you wake up. Focus on your breath, set a positive intention for the day, and visualize how you want your day to unfold.
- **Gratitude Practice:** Before getting out of bed, think of three things you are grateful for. This can shift your mindset towards positivity and appreciation.
- **Mindful Stretching:** Incorporate gentle stretching or yoga into your morning routine. Pay attention to your body's sensations and breathe deeply.

2. Mindful Eating

Eating mindfully involves being fully present during meals, savoring each bite, and appreciating the nourishment provided by your food. This practice can enhance your relationship with food and improve digestion. Try these tips:

- **Eliminate Distractions:** Turn off the TV, put away your phone, and focus solely on your meal.
- **Savor Each Bite:** Pay attention to the flavors, textures, and aromas of your food. Chew slowly and enjoy the experience.
- **Express Gratitude:** Take a moment before eating to express gratitude for your food and the effort that went into preparing it.

3. Mindful Breathing

Mindful breathing is a simple yet powerful practice that can be done anytime, anywhere. It helps to center your mind and reduce stress. Here's how to incorporate it into your day:

- **Regular Check-Ins:** Set a reminder to take a few deep breaths at regular intervals throughout the day. Focus on your breath as it flows in and out.

- **Stressful Moments:** Use mindful breathing during stressful situations to calm your mind and body. Inhale deeply through your nose, hold for a few seconds, and exhale slowly through your mouth.
- **Transition Times:** Practice mindful breathing during transitions, such as before starting a new task or after finishing a meeting. This can help you reset and refocus.

4. Mindful Walking

Walking mindfully turns a routine activity into a meditative practice. It's an excellent way to incorporate mindfulness into your daily life, especially if you spend a lot of time on your feet. Try these techniques:

- **Focus on Your Steps:** Pay attention to the sensation of your feet touching the ground with each step. Notice how your body moves and the rhythm of your walking.
- **Observe Your Surroundings:** Engage your senses by noticing the sights, sounds, and

smells around you. Appreciate the beauty of nature or the details of your environment.

- **Sync with Your Breath:** Coordinate your breath with your steps. For example, take a step with each inhale and exhale, creating a rhythmic and calming pattern.

5. Mindful Listening

Mindful listening involves giving your full attention to the speaker without interrupting or planning your response. It enhances communication and fosters deeper connections. Practice mindful listening by:

- **Being Present:** Focus solely on the speaker and what they are saying. Avoid distractions and make eye contact.
- **Non-Judgmental Attitude:** Listen without judging or forming opinions. Accept what the speaker is saying without immediately reacting.
- **Reflective Responses:** After the speaker finishes, reflect back what you heard to

ensure understanding. This shows you value their words and encourages open dialogue.

6. Mindful Technology Use

In our digital age, it's easy to get lost in screens and devices. Mindful technology use involves being aware of how and when we use technology, ensuring it enhances rather than detracts from our lives. Consider these practices:

- **Set Boundaries:** Establish specific times for checking emails, social media, and other digital activities. Avoid using devices during meals or before bed.
- **Single-Tasking:** Focus on one task at a time instead of multitasking. This can improve productivity and reduce stress.
- **Digital Detox:** Periodically disconnect from technology to recharge. Spend time in nature, engage in hobbies, or connect with loved ones face-to-face.

7. Mindful Work Practices

Bringing mindfulness into your work life can enhance productivity, reduce stress, and improve job satisfaction. Try incorporating these practices:

- **Mindful Planning:** Start your workday with a few minutes of mindful planning. Review your tasks, set priorities, and approach your work with intention.
- **Focus on One Task:** Practice single-tasking by focusing on one task at a time. Avoid constant task-switching, which can reduce efficiency and increase stress.
- **Mindful Breaks:** Take short, mindful breaks throughout the day. Step away from your desk, stretch, and practice deep breathing or a brief meditation.

8. Mindful Evening Routine

Ending the day with mindfulness can promote relaxation and better sleep. Consider these practices:

- **Reflect on Your Day:** Spend a few minutes reflecting on your day. Acknowledge your accomplishments, challenges, and what you are grateful for.
- **Evening Meditation:** Engage in a calming meditation or breathing exercise to unwind and prepare for sleep.
- **Disconnect from Technology:** Limit screen time in the hour before bed. Instead, read a book, take a warm bath, or practice gentle yoga.

Overcoming Challenges in Daily Mindfulness

1. Finding Time

Integrating mindfulness into a busy schedule can be challenging. Start with small, manageable practices and gradually increase their frequency and duration. Remember that even brief moments of mindfulness can make a significant impact.

2. Dealing with Distractions

Distractions are inevitable, but they can be managed. When you notice your mind wandering, gently bring your focus back to the present moment. Use reminders, such as alarms or visual cues, to prompt mindfulness throughout the day.

3. maintaining consistency

Consistency is key to reaping the benefits of mindfulness. Create a routine that works for you, and be patient with yourself. It's normal to miss a day or encounter setbacks. The important thing is to return to your practice without self-judgment.

CHAPTER 6

HEALTHY EXPRESSION OF EMOTIONS

Emotions are a fundamental aspect of the human experience, shaping our perceptions, influencing our decisions, and affecting our relationships. The ability to express emotions healthily is essential for emotional well-being, fostering positive relationships, and maintaining mental health. learning to express emotions in a healthy manner is crucial for transforming negativity into constructive outcomes.

The Importance of Healthy Emotional Expression

1. Mental Health and Well-being: Suppressing emotions can lead to increased stress, anxiety, and depression. Healthy emotional expression allows for emotional release, reducing the risk of mental health issues.

2. Improved Relationships: Open and honest communication of emotions fosters trust and understanding in relationships. It helps prevent misunderstandings and conflicts.

3. Personal Growth: Expressing emotions healthily enables self-reflection and personal insight. It promotes emotional intelligence and resilience.

4. Stress Reduction: Acknowledging and expressing emotions helps to alleviate the physiological and psychological stress associated with holding in feelings.

Barriers to Healthy Emotional Expression

1. Cultural and Societal Norms: Different cultures and societies have varying norms regarding emotional expression. Some may discourage open expression of certain emotions, leading individuals to suppress their feelings.

2. Fear of Judgment: Many people fear being judged or misunderstood if they express their emotions openly. This fear can lead to emotional suppression.

3. Lack of Emotional Awareness: Some individuals may struggle to identify and understand their emotions, making it difficult to express them healthily.

4. Past Experiences: Negative past experiences, such as trauma or rejection, can make individuals wary of expressing their emotions.

Strategies for Healthy Emotional Expression

1. Develop Emotional Awareness:
- **Identify Emotions:** Regularly check in with yourself to identify what you are feeling. Use

an emotion wheel or list of feelings to help pinpoint specific emotions.

- **Understand Triggers:** Reflect on what situations, people, or events trigger certain emotions. Understanding triggers can help you anticipate and manage your responses.

2. Practice Mindfulness:

- **Stay Present:** Use mindfulness techniques to stay present with your emotions. Observe them without judgment and let them pass naturally.
- **Breathing Exercises:** Practice deep breathing to calm your mind and body when you feel intense emotions. This can help you respond rather than react.

3. Communicate Openly:

- **Use "I" Statements:** Express your feelings using "I" statements to take ownership of your emotions. For example, say "I feel frustrated when…" instead of "You make me frustrated."

- **Be Specific:** Clearly articulate what you are feeling and why. Being specific helps others understand your perspective better.

4. Express Through Creative Outlets:
- **Journaling:** Writing about your emotions can help you process and understand them. It provides a private space to explore your feelings.
- **Art and Music:** Engage in creative activities such as drawing, painting, or playing music. These outlets can be powerful ways to express emotions without words.

5. Seek Support:
- **Talk to Trusted Individuals:** Share your feelings with friends, family, or a therapist. Talking about your emotions can provide relief and perspective.
- **Join Support Groups:** Participate in support groups where you can share experiences and feelings with others who understand.

6. Set Boundaries:

- **Know Your Limits:** Be aware of situations or people that drain your emotional energy. Set boundaries to protect your emotional well-being.
- **Say No:** Practice saying no when necessary to avoid overcommitting and becoming overwhelmed.

7. Engage in Physical Activity:

- **Exercise:** Physical activity is a great way to release pent-up emotions. Activities like running, yoga, or dancing can help you process feelings and reduce stress.
- **Mind-Body Practices:** Practices like tai chi or qigong combine physical movement with mindfulness, promoting emotional balance.
-

Healthy Expression in Relationships

1. Active Listening:

- **Be Present:** Give your full attention to the person speaking. Avoid interrupting or planning your response while they are talking.

- **Validate Feelings:** Acknowledge and validate the other person's feelings. Show empathy and understanding without immediately offering solutions.

2. Non-Defensive Communication:

- **Stay Calm:** When discussing difficult emotions, stay calm and composed. Avoid defensive reactions or blaming language.
- **Seek Resolution:** Focus on finding a resolution or understanding rather than winning an argument. Collaborate to address issues constructively.

3. Regular Check-Ins:

- **Open Dialogue:** Make it a habit to check in with your partner, family, or friends about your emotions. Encourage open dialogue and mutual support.
- **Express Appreciation:** Regularly express appreciation and gratitude for the people in your life. Positive emotions strengthen

relationships and create a supportive environment for discussing difficult feelings.

Healthy Expression at Work

1. Professional Boundaries:
- **Maintain Professionalism:** While it's important to express emotions, maintain professionalism. Choose appropriate times and settings to discuss feelings.
- **Use Constructive Feedback:** When addressing emotions related to work, frame your feedback constructively. Focus on behaviors and outcomes rather than personal attributes.

2. Stress Management:
- **Take Breaks:** Regularly take short breaks to manage stress and prevent burnout. Use these breaks to practice mindfulness or engage in relaxing activities.

- **Work-Life Balance:** Strive for a healthy work-life balance. Set boundaries between work and personal life to protect your emotional well-being.

3. Supportive Work Environment:

- **Promote Openness:** Encourage a culture of openness and support within your team. Create safe spaces for discussing emotions and stressors.
- **Employee Assistance Programs (EAPs):** Utilize available resources such as EAPs that offer counseling and support for emotional health.

Overcoming Challenges in Emotional Expression

1. Practice Self-Compassion:

- **Be Kind to Yourself:** Treat yourself with the same kindness and understanding that you would offer to a friend. Acknowledge that it's okay to feel and express emotions.
- **Forgive Yourself:** If you struggle with emotional expression, forgive yourself for past difficulties and focus on making positive changes.

2. Learn from Role Models:

- **Observe Others:** Learn from individuals who express their emotions healthily. Observe their techniques and incorporate them into your own practice.
- **Seek Guidance:** Don't hesitate to seek guidance from therapists, counselors, or mentors who can offer tools and strategies for healthy emotional expression.

3. Continuous Learning:

- **Stay Educated:** Continuously educate yourself about emotional intelligence and healthy expression. Read books, attend workshops, or take online courses.

- **Reflect and Adapt:** Regularly reflect on your emotional expression practices. Adapt and improve your strategies based on your experiences and feedback.

The Power of Journaling

Journaling is a powerful tool for emotional well-being and personal growth. It provides a structured way to explore thoughts and feelings, offering a safe space for reflection and self-expression. journaling is an invaluable practice for turning negativity into constructive outcomes.

The Benefits of Journaling

1. Emotional Release and Clarity: Journaling allows for the release of pent-up emotions, providing a healthy outlet for feelings that might otherwise remain bottled up. Writing about emotions helps clarify thoughts and understand complex feelings.

2. Stress Reduction: The act of writing can be therapeutic, reducing stress by allowing individuals to vent frustrations and worries. It creates a sense of relief and can be a form of mental decluttering.

3. Enhanced Self-Awareness: Journaling fosters self-awareness by encouraging individuals to reflect on their thoughts and behaviors. It helps identify patterns and recurring themes, contributing to a deeper understanding of oneself.

4. Improved Problem-Solving: Writing about challenges and problems can lead to new perspectives and solutions. The process of articulating issues on paper often brings clarity and reveals actionable steps.

5. Emotional Regulation: Regular journaling promotes emotional regulation by providing a consistent practice for processing and managing emotions. It helps individuals recognize and address negative emotions before they escalate.

6. Personal Growth and Development: Journaling supports personal growth by encouraging continuous self-reflection and introspection. It provides a record of progress, allowing individuals to track their growth over time.

7. Boosted Creativity: The act of writing stimulates creativity, allowing individuals to explore ideas and thoughts freely. It can be particularly beneficial for those seeking to unlock their creative potential.

Different Types of Journaling

1. Reflective Journaling: This involves reflecting on daily experiences, thoughts, and emotions. It's a way to process what happened during the day and how it made you feel.

2. Gratitude Journaling: Focusing on gratitude involves writing down things you are thankful for. This practice can shift focus from negative to positive aspects of life, fostering a more optimistic outlook.

3. Bullet Journaling: This method combines traditional journaling with to-do lists, habit tracking, and goal setting. It's a flexible system that can be customized to fit individual needs.

4. Creative Journaling: This type of journaling incorporates elements of art, such as drawing, painting, or collage, alongside written entries. It's a way to explore emotions and thoughts through multiple mediums.

5. Dream Journaling: Recording dreams can provide insights into the subconscious mind. This type of journaling can be particularly useful for those interested in understanding their deeper thoughts and feelings.

6. Prompted Journaling: Using prompts or questions to guide writing can help focus thoughts and explore specific topics. Prompts can range from introspective questions to hypothetical scenarios.

How to Start a Journaling Practice

1. Choose Your Medium: Decide whether you prefer a physical journal or a digital one. Some people enjoy the tactile experience of writing by hand, while others prefer the convenience of typing on a computer or using a journaling app.

2. Set a Regular Schedule: Consistency is key to reaping the benefits of journaling. Set aside a specific time each day or week for journaling. It could be in the morning to set intentions for the day or in the evening to reflect on the day's events.

3. Create a Comfortable Space: Find a quiet, comfortable place where you can write without distractions. This could be a cozy corner of your home, a café, or a park.

4. Start with Prompts: If you're unsure what to write about, start with prompts. These can be questions like, "What am I feeling right now?" or "What am I grateful for today?"

5. Write Freely: Don't worry about grammar, spelling, or structure. Allow your thoughts to flow freely onto the page. The goal is to express yourself, not to create a polished piece of writing.

6. **Be Honest:** Authenticity is crucial in journaling. Write honestly about your thoughts and feelings, even if they are difficult or uncomfortable. This honesty is where true self-discovery happens.

7. Review and Reflect: Periodically review your journal entries. Reflecting on past entries can provide insights into patterns, growth, and areas that may need more attention.

Overcoming Common Challenges

1. Finding Time: Many people struggle to find time for journaling. Start with just a few minutes a day and gradually increase the duration. Integrating journaling into your daily routine can make it a natural habit.

2. Writer's Block: If you experience writer's block, use prompts or questions to get started. Remember, there's no right or wrong way to journal. Write about whatever comes to mind.

3. Fear of Judgment: Journaling is a private activity, so let go of the fear of judgment. Your journal is for your eyes only, providing a safe space to express your true feelings without criticism.

4. Perfectionism: Don't strive for perfection in your journaling. The purpose is to express and explore your thoughts and emotions, not to produce flawless writing. Embrace imperfections as part of the process.

Journaling Techniques for Turning Negative Emotions into Positive Growth

1. Stream of Consciousness Writing: This involves writing continuously without worrying about coherence or structure. It's a way to release whatever is on your mind, helping to process emotions and thoughts.

2. Letter Writing: Write letters to yourself or others, expressing feelings that you might find difficult to articulate in person. These letters can be kept private or shared if you choose.

3. Positive Affirmations: Write positive affirmations to counter negative thoughts and emotions. This practice can help shift your mindset and foster a more positive outlook.

4. Emotion Tracking: Keep track of your emotions over time, noting triggers and patterns. This can help you understand what influences your mood and how to manage it better.

5. Visualization: Describe your ideal emotional state or a positive future scenario. Visualization can inspire hope and motivate you to work towards your goals.

The Transformative Power of Journaling

Journaling is not just a tool for Turning Negative Emotions into Positive Growth; it's a transformative practice that can lead to profound personal growth. By consistently engaging in journaling, individuals can:

1. Develop Emotional Resilience: Regularly processing and expressing emotions builds resilience, making it easier to navigate challenges and setbacks.

2. Cultivate Self-Compassion: Journaling encourages self-compassion by providing a space to acknowledge and validate your feelings. It helps in developing a kinder, more understanding relationship with yourself.

3. Enhance Empathy: Understanding your own emotions can improve your ability to empathize with others. Journaling can foster greater emotional intelligence and interpersonal skills.

4. Achieve Goals: Setting and tracking goals in your journal can provide motivation and accountability. It helps in breaking down larger objectives into manageable steps.

5. Create a Legacy: Journals can serve as a record of your thoughts, experiences, and growth. They can be a valuable resource for reflecting on your journey and sharing your story with others.

Effective Communication Skills

Effective communication skills are essential for navigating life's challenges, building strong relationships, and achieving personal and professional goals. mastering communication skills is crucial for expressing emotions constructively and fostering understanding. This chapter explores the components of effective communication, the barriers that impede it, and strategies to enhance these skills.

The Components of Effective Communication

1. Active Listening: Active listening involves fully focusing on the speaker, understanding their message, and responding thoughtfully. It requires paying attention, not just to the words but also to the tone, body language, and emotions behind the message.

2. Clarity and Conciseness: Clear and concise communication ensures that the message is easily understood. Avoiding jargon, using simple language, and being direct helps prevent misunderstandings.

3. Nonverbal Communication: Nonverbal cues, such as facial expressions, gestures, posture, and eye contact, play a significant role in communication. These cues can reinforce or contradict the spoken message, so being aware of them is vital.

4. Empathy: Empathy involves understanding and sharing the feelings of others. Communicating with empathy means acknowledging the emotions and perspectives of others, which helps build trust and rapport.

5. Open-Mindedness: Being open-minded in communication means being willing to consider different viewpoints and ideas. It fosters a collaborative and respectful dialogue.

6. Feedback: Providing and receiving feedback is an integral part of effective communication. Constructive feedback helps individuals understand how their message is received and how they can improve their communication skills.

7. Adaptability: Effective communicators adapt their style to suit different contexts and audiences. This flexibility ensures that the message is appropriate and well-received.

Barriers to Effective Communication

1. Emotional Barriers: Strong emotions like anger, fear, or frustration can hinder effective communication. They can lead to misinterpretations and defensive reactions.

2. Physical Barriers: Environmental factors, such as noise, distance, and physical obstacles, can disrupt communication. Ensuring a conducive environment is essential for clear communication.

3. Language Barriers: Differences in language, jargon, or terminology can cause misunderstandings. Using simple and clear language can help bridge these gaps.

4. Cultural Barriers: Cultural differences in communication styles, norms, and values can create misunderstandings. Being culturally aware and respectful is crucial for effective cross-cultural communication.

5. Perceptual Barriers: Individual perceptions and biases can influence how messages are interpreted. Recognizing and addressing these biases is important for clear communication.

6. Lack of Attention: Distracted or inattentive listening can lead to misunderstandings. Active listening requires full attention and engagement.

7. Assumptions and Jumping to Conclusions: Making assumptions or jumping to conclusions without verifying information can distort the message. Clarifying and confirming details is essential.

Strategies to Enhance Communication Skills

1. Practice Active Listening:

- **Focus on the Speaker:** Give your full attention to the speaker. Avoid distractions and make eye contact to show engagement.
- **Use Reflective Listening:** Paraphrase or summarize what the speaker has said to ensure understanding. This technique also shows that you are actively listening and valuing their input.
- **Ask Questions:** Asking open-ended questions encourages the speaker to elaborate and provides more context.

2. Be Clear and Concise:

- **Organize Your Thoughts:** Before speaking, organize your thoughts to ensure clarity. Think about the main points you want to convey.

- **Avoid Jargon:** Use simple and straightforward language. Avoid technical jargon or complex terms unless necessary, and provide explanations when needed.
- **Stick to the Point:** Be concise and stay focused on the topic. Avoid unnecessary details that might confuse the message.

3. Enhance Nonverbal Communication:
- **Be Mindful of Body Language:** Ensure that your body language aligns with your message. Open and relaxed postures, appropriate gestures, and facial expressions enhance communication.
- **Maintain Eye Contact:** Eye contact shows attentiveness and sincerity. However, be mindful of cultural differences regarding eye contact.
- **Pay Attention to Tone and Pitch:** Your tone and pitch can convey emotions and attitudes. Aim for a tone that matches the message and is respectful.

4. Cultivate Empathy:

- **Acknowledge Emotions:** Recognize and validate the emotions of others. Phrases like "I understand how you feel" can show empathy and build connection.
- **Put Yourself in Their Shoes:** Try to see the situation from the other person's perspective. This understanding can foster compassion and improve communication.

5. Stay Open-Minded:

- **Welcome Different Perspectives:** Be open to hearing different viewpoints. Encourage others to share their thoughts and listen without judgment.
- **Avoid Interrupting:** Let the speaker finish before responding. Interruptions can be seen as disrespectful and hinder open dialogue.

6. Give and Receive Feedback:

- **Be Constructive:** When providing feedback, focus on specific behaviors rather than personal attributes. Use "I" statements to express your observations and feelings.

- **Accept Feedback Gracefully:** When receiving feedback, listen without becoming defensive. Consider the feedback objectively and use it for personal growth.

7. Adapt to Your Audience:

- **Know Your Audience:** Consider the background, knowledge, and expectations of your audience. Tailor your message to suit their needs and level of understanding.
- **Be Flexible:** Be prepared to adjust your communication style based on the situation and feedback from your audience.

Effective Communication in Different Contexts

1. Personal Relationships:

- **Express Emotions Openly:** Share your feelings and thoughts honestly with your partner, family, or friends. Honest communication fosters trust and intimacy.

- **Resolve Conflicts Constructively:** Address conflicts directly and calmly. Use "I" statements and focus on finding mutually beneficial solutions.

2. Workplace Communication:

- **Collaborate and Share Ideas:** Encourage open communication and collaboration with colleagues. Share ideas and feedback constructively to enhance teamwork.
- **Communicate Expectations Clearly:** Ensure that expectations and goals are clearly communicated to avoid misunderstandings and ensure alignment.

3. Cross-Cultural Communication:

- **Respect Cultural Differences:** Be aware of and respect cultural differences in communication styles and norms. Adapt your communication approach to suit different cultural contexts.
- **Learn About Other Cultures:** Take the time to learn about the cultures of the people you are communicating with. This knowledge can

help prevent misunderstandings and build rapport.

4. Digital Communication:

- **Use Clear and Professional Language:** In emails, messages, and other digital communications, use clear and professional language. Avoid slang or overly casual language unless appropriate.
- **Be Mindful of Tone:** Without nonverbal cues, the tone can be easily misunderstood in written communication. Be mindful of how your message might be interpreted and use emojis or clarifying statements if necessary.

Building Communication Skills Over Time

1. Practice Regularly:

- **Engage in Conversations:** Practice your communication skills in daily interactions. Engage in conversations with a variety of people to build confidence and adaptability.
- **Join Public Speaking Groups:** Groups like Toastmasters provide a supportive

environment to practice public speaking and receive constructive feedback.

2. Seek Feedback:

- **Ask for Feedback:** Request feedback from trusted individuals about your communication skills. Use their insights to identify areas for improvement.
- **Reflect on Feedback:** Reflect on the feedback you receive and consider how you can apply it to enhance your communication skills.

3. Study Communication Techniques:

- **Read Books and Articles:** There are many resources available on effective communication. Reading books and articles can provide new techniques and perspectives.
- **Attend Workshops and Seminars:** Participate in workshops and seminars focused on communication skills. These events offer practical exercises and expert guidance.

4. Observe Effective Communicators:

- **Learn from Role Models:** Observe individuals who are skilled communicators. Note their techniques and approaches, and consider how you can incorporate them into your own practice.
- **Analyze Public Speakers:** Watch public speakers and analyze their communication style. Pay attention to how they engage their audience and convey their message.

CHAPTER 7

PHYSICAL ACTIVITIES FOR EMOTIONAL RELIEF

Physical activity is a powerful and often underappreciated tool for managing and alleviating negative emotions. Engaging in regular physical exercise not only benefits physical health but also plays a crucial role in enhancing emotional well-being. This chapter explores the various ways physical activities can provide emotional relief, the science behind their effectiveness, and practical strategies for incorporating them into daily life.

The Connection Between Physical Activity and Emotional Health

1. Release of Endorphins: Physical activity stimulates the production of endorphins, often referred to as "feel-good" hormones. These chemicals interact with receptors in the brain to reduce the perception of pain and trigger positive feelings, akin to the effects of morphine.

2. Reduction of Stress Hormones: Exercise helps lower levels of stress hormones such as cortisol and adrenaline. Lowering these hormones can lead to a calmer, more relaxed state of mind.

3. Improved Sleep: Regular physical activity can improve the quality of sleep, which is essential for emotional regulation. Better sleep reduces irritability, enhances mood, and improves overall mental health.

4. Increased Self-Esteem and Confidence: Achieving fitness goals and maintaining a regular exercise routine can boost self-esteem and confidence. The sense of accomplishment from physical activity can improve one's outlook on life.

5. Enhanced Brain Function: Exercise increases blood flow to the brain and promotes the growth of new brain cells, particularly in the hippocampus, which is involved in mood regulation and memory. This leads to improved cognitive function and emotional stability.

Types of Physical Activities for Emotional Relief

1. Aerobic Exercises:
- **Running and Jogging:** These activities are excellent for releasing endorphins and improving cardiovascular health. They also offer time for personal reflection.
- **Cycling:** Whether on a stationary bike or outdoors, cycling can be a meditative

experience that reduces stress and enhances mood.

- **Swimming:** Swimming combines the benefits of aerobic exercise with the calming effects of being in water. It's a full-body workout that can also be soothing for the mind.

2. Strength Training:

- **Weightlifting:** Strength training increases muscle mass and strength, which can improve physical appearance and self-esteem. It also provides a sense of control and accomplishment.
- **Resistance Band Exercises:** These are a versatile way to build strength and can be done at home or in a gym, making them accessible for many people.

3. Mind-Body Exercises:

- **Yoga:** Yoga combines physical postures, breathing exercises, and meditation to promote relaxation and emotional balance.

It's effective for reducing anxiety and enhancing mindfulness.
- **Tai Chi:** This ancient martial art focuses on slow, deliberate movements and deep breathing. It's known for its stress-reducing and meditative qualities.

4. Recreational Activities:
- **Dancing:** Dancing is a fun way to engage in physical activity and express emotions. It's also a social activity that can reduce feelings of isolation.
- **Hiking:** Being in nature while hiking can have a profound impact on mental health. The combination of physical exertion and the calming effects of nature reduces stress and improves mood.
- **Team Sports:** Sports like soccer, basketball, or volleyball promote physical fitness and provide social interaction, teamwork, and a sense of community.

5. Low-Impact Exercises:

- Walking: Walking is a simple, accessible form of exercise that can be done almost anywhere. Regular walks can significantly reduce stress and improve mood.
- **Pilates:** Pilates focuses on core strength, flexibility, and mindful movement. It's beneficial for improving physical and mental resilience.

Incorporating Physical Activity into Daily Life

1. Set Realistic Goals: Start with achievable fitness goals that fit your lifestyle and fitness level. Setting small, incremental goals can help maintain motivation and build a sustainable exercise habit.

2. Create a Routine: Schedule regular workout times and treat them as non-negotiable appointments. Consistency is key to reaping the emotional benefits of physical activity.

3. Find Activities You Enjoy: Choose activities that you find enjoyable and engaging. When exercise feels like a chore, it's harder to stay committed. Mixing up activities can also prevent boredom.

4. Incorporate Social Elements: Exercise with friends or join a fitness group or class. The social aspect of physical activity can provide additional emotional support and motivation.

5. Use Technology: Fitness apps, wearable trackers, and online workout programs can provide guidance, track progress, and keep you motivated. Many apps offer virtual communities for additional support.

6. Practice Mindfulness During Exercise: Pay attention to your body and how it feels during exercise. This mindfulness can enhance the emotional benefits of physical activity by helping you stay present and focused.

7. **Combine with Other Healthy Habits:** Pairing exercise with other healthy habits, such as balanced nutrition, adequate sleep, and hydration, amplifies the overall benefits for emotional well-being.

Overcoming Barriers to Physical Activity

1. Lack of Time: Integrate physical activity into your daily routine by taking short, active breaks, walking or biking to work, or doing quick home workouts. Prioritize exercise by scheduling it into your calendar.

2. Physical Limitations: Choose low-impact activities that are easier on the joints, such as swimming, cycling, or yoga. Consult with a healthcare provider to design a safe exercise plan that accommodates your needs.

3. Motivation: Set specific, measurable goals and track your progress. Reward yourself for reaching milestones, and remind yourself of the emotional and physical benefits of exercise.

4. Cost: Exercise doesn't have to be expensive. There are many free or low-cost options, such as walking, running, bodyweight exercises, or using online workout videos. Community centers often offer affordable fitness classes.

5. Fear of Judgment: Focus on your personal goals and progress rather than comparing yourself to others. Remember that everyone's fitness journey is unique, and most people are supportive and encouraging.

6. Weather and Environment: Adapt your workout routine to suit different weather conditions. Indoor activities, such as gym workouts, home exercises, or swimming in an indoor pool, can keep you active regardless of the weather.

The Connection Between Body and Mind

Understanding the connection between body and mind is essential for Turning Negative Emotions into Positive Growth and achieving holistic well-being. This chapter delves into the intricate relationship between physical and mental health, exploring how the state of one impacts the other, and offers strategies for harnessing this connection to enhance emotional resilience and well-being.

The Science Behind the Body-Mind Connection

1. The Brain-Body Communication Network: The brain and body are connected through a complex communication network involving the nervous, endocrine, and immune systems. This network allows for constant feedback and interaction between physical and mental states.

2. Neurotransmitters and Hormones: Neurotransmitters (like serotonin, dopamine, and norepinephrine) and hormones (such as cortisol and adrenaline) play a crucial role in regulating mood, emotions, and physical responses. Physical activity, nutrition, and stress management can influence the levels of these chemicals, impacting both mental and physical health.

3. The Role of the Vagus Nerve: The vagus nerve, a key part of the parasympathetic nervous system, connects the brain to various organs, including the heart, lungs, and digestive tract. It plays a significant role in regulating stress responses and promoting relaxation.

4. The Gut-Brain Axis: The gut and brain communicate bidirectionally through the gut-brain axis, involving the vagus nerve, immune system, and gut microbiota. A healthy gut microbiome can positively influence mood and cognitive function, while gut imbalances can contribute to mental health issues.

How Physical Health Impacts Mental Health

1. Physical Activity and Mood Enhancement:
- **Exercise and Endorphins:** Physical activity stimulates the production of endorphins, which are natural mood lifters. Regular exercise can reduce symptoms of anxiety and depression.
- **Improved Sleep:** Exercise promotes better sleep quality, which is essential for emotional regulation. Poor sleep can exacerbate negative emotions and mental health issues.

2. Nutrition and Mental Health:
- **Balanced Diet:** A diet rich in whole foods, including fruits, vegetables, lean proteins, and healthy fats, supports brain health. Nutrients like omega-3 fatty acids, B

vitamins, and antioxidants play a vital role in cognitive function and mood regulation.

- **Hydration:** Staying hydrated is crucial for optimal brain function. Dehydration can lead to fatigue, irritability, and cognitive decline.

3. Stress Management:

- **Chronic Stress:** Prolonged stress can negatively impact physical health, leading to conditions such as hypertension, weakened immune function, and metabolic disorders. These physical issues can, in turn, exacerbate mental health problems.
- **Relaxation Techniques:** Practices such as deep breathing, meditation, and yoga activate the parasympathetic nervous system, reducing stress and promoting mental calmness.

4. Sleep and Emotional Well-Being:

- **Sleep Deprivation:** Lack of sleep can impair cognitive function, decision-making, and emotional regulation. It increases the risk of developing anxiety and depression.

- **Healthy Sleep Habits:** Establishing a regular sleep routine, creating a restful environment, and avoiding stimulants before bedtime can improve sleep quality and support mental health.

How Mental Health Impacts Physical Health

1. Emotional Stress and Physical Symptoms:
- **Psychosomatic Symptoms:** Emotional stress can manifest physically through symptoms such as headaches, muscle tension, digestive issues, and fatigue. Addressing the underlying emotional causes can alleviate these physical symptoms.
- **Chronic Conditions:** Mental health issues like chronic anxiety and depression can increase the risk of developing chronic physical conditions, including cardiovascular disease and diabetes.

2. Behavioral Impact:

- **Healthy Habits:** Positive mental health promotes healthy behaviors such as regular exercise, balanced nutrition, and adequate sleep. Conversely, poor mental health can lead to unhealthy behaviors like overeating, substance abuse, and sedentary lifestyle.
- **Self-Care:** Mental health struggles can reduce motivation for self-care activities, exacerbating physical health issues.

3. Immune System Function:

- **Stress and Immunity:** Chronic stress weakens the immune system, making the body more susceptible to infections and illnesses. Reducing stress through mental health interventions can strengthen immune function.
- **Inflammation:** Mental health conditions like depression are associated with increased inflammation in the body, which can contribute to various physical health problems.

Strategies for Enhancing the Body-Mind Connection

1. Regular Physical Activity:

- **Exercise Routine:** Incorporate aerobic exercises, strength training, and mind-body practices into your routine. Aim for at least 150 minutes of moderate-intensity exercise per week.
- **Enjoyable Activities:** Choose physical activities that you enjoy to increase adherence and motivation. Activities like dancing, hiking, or team sports can be both fun and beneficial.

2. Balanced Nutrition:

- **Whole Foods:** Focus on a diet rich in whole, unprocessed foods. Include a variety of fruits, vegetables, lean proteins, and healthy fats.
- **Mindful Eating:** Practice mindful eating by paying attention to hunger and fullness cues, eating slowly, and savoring each bite. This

can improve digestion and emotional satisfaction with meals.

3. Stress Management Techniques:

- **Mindfulness Meditation:** Incorporate mindfulness meditation into your daily routine. Even a few minutes of meditation can reduce stress and enhance emotional regulation.
- **Relaxation Exercises:** Practice deep breathing, progressive muscle relaxation, or guided imagery to activate the parasympathetic nervous system and promote relaxation.

4. Adequate Sleep:

- **Sleep Hygiene:** Establish a regular sleep schedule, create a calming bedtime routine, and ensure a comfortable sleep environment.
- **Limit Stimulants:** Avoid caffeine, alcohol, and heavy meals close to bedtime. Limit screen time before bed to reduce blue light exposure.

5. Healthy Relationships:

- **Social Support:** Cultivate and maintain healthy relationships with friends, family, and community. Social support is crucial for emotional well-being and can buffer against stress.
- **Effective Communication:** Practice effective communication skills to enhance relationships and reduce conflicts. Expressing emotions and needs clearly can prevent misunderstandings and promote emotional health.

6. Professional Help:

- **Therapy and Counseling:** Seek professional help from therapists or counselors when needed. Therapy can provide tools for managing stress, anxiety, and depression.
- **Medical Consultation:** Regular check-ups with healthcare providers ensure that both physical and mental health needs are addressed. Open communication with your doctor about mental health is important for holistic care.

Integrating Body-Mind Practices into Daily Life

1. Mindful Movement:
- **Yoga:** Practice yoga to integrate physical movement with mindfulness. Yoga enhances flexibility, strength, and mental clarity.
- **Tai Chi and Qigong:** These gentle martial arts focus on slow, deliberate movements and deep breathing, promoting relaxation and mental focus.

2. Nature and Outdoors:
- **Nature Walks:** Spend time in nature to reduce stress and improve mood. Walking in natural settings has been shown to lower cortisol levels and enhance emotional well-being.
- **Gardening:** Gardening can be a therapeutic activity that combines physical activity with the calming effects of nature.

3. Creative Expression:

- **Art and Music:** Engage in creative activities like drawing, painting, or playing an instrument. These activities can serve as emotional outlets and reduce stress.
- **Writing:** Journaling or creative writing allows for emotional expression and reflection, promoting mental clarity and emotional relief.

4. Gratitude Practice:

- **Gratitude Journals:** Keep a gratitude journal to regularly reflect on positive aspects of life. Focusing on gratitude can shift attention away from negative emotions and improve overall mood.
- **Expressing Thanks:** Regularly express gratitude to others, enhancing social connections and emotional well-being.

5. Routine and Structure:

- **Daily Schedule:** Establish a balanced daily routine that includes time for physical activity, relaxation, social interaction, and personal hobbies.

- **Goal Setting:** Set realistic and achievable goals for both physical and mental health. Tracking progress can provide a sense of accomplishment and motivation.

Success Stories and Personal Accounts

1. Sarah's Transformation Through Yoga: Sarah struggled with anxiety and chronic stress. She started practicing yoga regularly and found that the combination of physical postures, breathing exercises, and meditation significantly reduced her anxiety levels and improved her overall sense of well-being.

2. Mike's Journey to Better Health: Mike faced depression and weight gain after a major life change. By integrating regular exercise, balanced nutrition, and mindfulness meditation into his daily routine, he managed to lose weight, improve his mood, and regain his zest for life.

3. Linda's Path to Emotional Balance: Linda, who dealt with chronic pain and emotional stress, discovered the benefits of tai chi. The gentle movements and focus on breath work helped her manage pain, reduce stress, and enhance her emotional resilience.

4. John's Holistic Approach to Wellness: John, who had a high-stress job, implemented a holistic approach by incorporating physical activity, healthy eating, mindfulness, and regular therapy sessions into his life. This multifaceted strategy improved his physical health, reduced stress, and enhanced his overall emotional well-being.

Exercise and Endorphins

Exercise is not only beneficial for physical health but also plays a significant role in enhancing mental well-being. One of the key mechanisms behind this is the release of endorphins, often referred to as "feel-good" hormones. This chapter delves into the science behind exercise and endorphins, how they impact emotional health, and practical ways to incorporate exercise into your routine to harness these benefits.

Understanding Endorphins

1. What Are Endorphins?
- **Definition:** Endorphins are a group of peptide hormones produced by the central nervous system and the pituitary gland. They function as neurotransmitters, helping to transmit signals within the nervous system.
- **Role:** Endorphins are primarily known for their ability to reduce pain and induce feelings of pleasure or euphoria. They are part of the body's natural pain relief system and are often released in response to stress or discomfort.

2. The Biochemical Process:

- **Production:** Endorphins are produced in response to various stimuli, including physical exercise, pain, stress, and even certain foods. When released, they bind to opioid receptors in the brain, which helps to block pain signals.
- **Effects:** The binding of endorphins to these receptors not only reduces the perception of pain but also triggers the release of dopamine, another neurotransmitter associated with pleasure and reward.

The Impact of Exercise on Endorphin Levels

1. Types of Exercise:
- **Aerobic Exercise:** Activities like running, cycling, and swimming are particularly effective at increasing endorphin levels. These exercises involve sustained physical activity that elevates the heart rate and promotes cardiovascular health.
- **Strength Training:** Weightlifting and resistance exercises also stimulate endorphin production. These activities build muscle

strength and endurance, contributing to overall physical and mental well-being.

- **High-Intensity Interval Training (HIIT):** HIIT involves short bursts of intense exercise followed by periods of rest. This type of exercise is highly effective in boosting endorphin levels in a relatively short amount of time.

2. Duration and Intensity:

- **Short-Term Effects:** Even a short, intense workout can lead to a noticeable increase in endorphin levels. For example, a 20-minute run or a quick HIIT session can provide a significant mood boost.
- **Long-Term Effects:** Regular, consistent exercise leads to sustained higher levels of endorphins and other mood-enhancing neurotransmitters. This ongoing production helps maintain a positive mood and reduce the risk of mental health issues over time.

3. Exercise-Induced Euphoria:

- **Runner's High:** One of the most well-known examples of endorphin release is the "runner's high." This phenomenon is characterized by a state of euphoria and reduced anxiety after prolonged aerobic exercise. It is attributed to the surge in endorphins and other neurotransmitters.
- **Mental Clarity and Focus:** Beyond euphoria, exercise can improve mental clarity and focus. Endorphins, along with other brain chemicals released during exercise, enhance cognitive function and promote a sense of mental alertness.

Psychological Benefits of Endorphin Release

1. **Mood Enhancement:**
   - **Reduction in Anxiety and Depression:** Endorphins act as natural mood lifters, helping to reduce symptoms of anxiety and depression. Regular exercise can be as

effective as medication for some individuals in managing mild to moderate depression.

- **Stress Relief:** Exercise helps reduce levels of stress hormones like cortisol while increasing endorphin levels. This dual effect leads to a more balanced emotional state and better stress management.

2. Improved Self-Esteem:

- **Body Image:** Regular exercise can improve physical appearance and fitness, leading to enhanced self-esteem and body image. This positive self-perception contributes to overall emotional well-being.

- **Sense of Accomplishment:** Setting and achieving fitness goals provides a sense of accomplishment and boosts confidence. The endorphin release during and after exercise reinforces these positive feelings.

3. Enhanced Social Interaction:

- **Group Activities:** Participating in group exercise classes or team sports fosters social interaction and community support. The social aspect of exercise can further enhance mood and reduce feelings of isolation.

- **Motivation and Accountability:** Exercising with others provides motivation and accountability, making it easier to maintain a regular exercise routine and experience the associated endorphin benefits.

Practical Strategies for Maximizing Endorphin Benefits

1. Creating an Exercise Routine:

- **Consistency:** Aim to exercise regularly, ideally most days of the week. Consistency is key to maintaining elevated endorphin levels and reaping long-term mental health benefits.
- **Variety:** Incorporate a variety of exercises to keep workouts interesting and engaging. Mixing aerobic activities, strength training, and flexibility exercises can prevent boredom and promote overall fitness.

2. Setting Realistic Goals:

- **Short-Term Goals:** Set achievable short-term goals to maintain motivation and experience regular endorphin boosts. These goals could include completing a specific workout, running a certain distance, or achieving a new personal best.
- **Long-Term Goals:** Establish long-term fitness goals to work towards over time. These might include training for a race, increasing strength, or improving overall health markers.

3. Mindfulness and Enjoyment:

- **Mindful Exercise:** Pay attention to your body and how it feels during exercise. Being mindful can enhance the experience and increase the release of endorphins.
- **Fun Activities:** Choose activities you enjoy to ensure exercise remains a pleasurable and sustainable habit. Whether it's dancing, hiking, or playing a sport, find what brings you joy.

4. Incorporating Social Elements:

- **Workout Buddies:** Exercise with friends or family members to combine physical activity with social interaction. This can make workouts more enjoyable and provide additional emotional support.
- **Group Classes:** Join group exercise classes or sports teams to benefit from the collective energy and camaraderie. The shared experience can amplify the endorphin release and overall enjoyment.

5. Tracking Progress:

- **Fitness Apps:** Use fitness apps or wearable devices to track your workouts, monitor progress, and set new goals. Tracking can provide motivation and a sense of accomplishment.
- **Journaling:** Keep an exercise journal to document your workouts, reflect on how you feel after exercising, and track improvements in mood and physical fitness over time.

Overcoming Barriers to Exercise

1. **Time Constraints:**
   - **Short Workouts:** Even short workouts can be effective. High-Intensity Interval Training (HIIT) and other quick routines can fit into a busy schedule and provide significant endorphin boosts.
   - **Active Breaks:** Incorporate physical activity into your daily routine with active breaks, such as taking the stairs, walking during lunch breaks, or doing quick exercises at your desk.

2. **Lack of Motivation:**
   - **Find Your Why:** Identify personal reasons for exercising, whether it's improving health, boosting mood, or enjoying a hobby. Having a clear purpose can enhance motivation.
   - **Rewards and Incentives:** Reward yourself for reaching fitness milestones. Treat yourself to something enjoyable, like a favorite activity or a relaxing bath, after completing a workout.

3. Physical Limitations:

- **Low-Impact Exercises:** Choose low-impact activities like swimming, cycling, or yoga that are gentler on the joints. These exercises can still provide significant endorphin benefits without straining the body.
- **Professional Guidance:** Consult with a healthcare provider or fitness professional to design a safe and effective exercise plan tailored to your abilities and limitations.

4. Environmental Factors:

- **Indoor Options:** Have indoor workout options for times when weather or other factors prevent outdoor exercise. Home workouts, gym sessions, or indoor classes can ensure consistency.
- **Creative Spaces:** Utilize available spaces creatively, such as using living room furniture for bodyweight exercises or finding local community centers for indoor activities.

Success Stories and Personal Accounts

1. Emily's Endorphin Boost Through Running: Emily struggled with chronic stress and low mood. She started running regularly and noticed a significant improvement in her mental state. The endorphin release from her runs provided a natural mood boost, helping her manage stress and feel more positive.

2. Jake's Journey with Weightlifting: Jake faced depression and low self-esteem. He began strength training and found that the physical improvements and endorphin release during workouts enhanced his confidence and overall mood. Weightlifting became a vital part of his mental health routine.

3. Sophia's Yoga Transformation: Sophia dealt with anxiety and sleep issues. She incorporated yoga into her daily routine and experienced the calming effects of endorphin release. The combination of physical postures and mindfulness in yoga helped her achieve emotional balance and better sleep.

4. David's Social Exercise Experience: David felt isolated after moving to a new city. He joined a

local soccer team and discovered the dual benefits of physical exercise and social interaction. The endorphin boost from playing soccer and the camaraderie with teammates significantly improved his mood and sense of belonging.

CHAPTER 8

BUILDING A SUPPORT SYSTEM

A strong support system is crucial for Turning Negative Emotions into Positive Growth and fostering emotional well-being. This chapter explores the importance of a support system, the different types of support available, and practical steps to build and maintain a robust network of supportive relationships.

The Importance of a Support System

1. Emotional Support:

- **Validation and Empathy:** Emotional support involves receiving validation and empathy from others. This helps individuals feel understood and accepted, which can significantly reduce feelings of isolation and loneliness.
- **Stress Relief:** Sharing emotions and experiences with supportive people can alleviate stress. Knowing that someone is there to listen and provide comfort can make challenging situations more manageable.

2. Practical Assistance:

- **Help with Tasks:** Practical support includes assistance with daily tasks and responsibilities. This can range from help with household chores to providing childcare, which can reduce the burden on individuals experiencing emotional distress.
- **Resource Sharing:** Supportive individuals can share valuable resources, such as information about mental health services, community programs, and coping strategies.

3. Social Interaction:

- **Building Connections:** Regular social interaction with supportive people fosters a sense of belonging and community. This connection is vital for emotional health and can combat feelings of isolation.
- **Positive Influence:** Being around positive and supportive individuals can influence one's outlook and behavior, promoting healthier coping mechanisms and emotional resilience.

4. Encouragement and Motivation:

- **Goal Achievement:** A support system can provide encouragement and motivation to achieve personal and professional goals. Supportive individuals can offer guidance, celebrate successes, and provide a sense of accountability.
- **Resilience Building:** Encouragement from others can bolster resilience, helping individuals bounce back from setbacks and maintain a positive attitude in the face of adversity.

Types of Support

1. Family:

- **Immediate Family:** Parents, siblings, and children can provide a strong foundation of support. These relationships are often based on long-term bonds and deep emotional connections.
- **Extended Family:** Extended family members, such as aunts, uncles, and cousins, can also offer valuable support and contribute to a broader support network.

2. Friends:

- **Close Friends:** Trusted friends provide emotional support, companionship, and practical assistance. These relationships are often based on mutual understanding and shared experiences.
- **Acquaintances:** While not as close as best friends, acquaintances can still offer valuable support, especially in specific areas such as work or hobbies.

3. Community:

- **Local Groups:** Community groups, such as clubs, organizations, and support groups, offer a sense of belonging and collective support. These groups can be based on shared interests, values, or experiences.
- **Online Communities:** Online support groups and forums provide a platform for connecting with others who share similar experiences. These virtual communities can offer valuable emotional support and resources.

4. Professional Support:

- **Therapists and Counselors:** Mental health professionals provide expert guidance and support for Turning Negative Emotions into Positive Growth and developing coping strategies. Regular sessions with a therapist can be a cornerstone of a strong support system.
- **Healthcare Providers:** Doctors, nurses, and other healthcare professionals offer medical

support and can provide referrals to mental health services and community resources.

5. Spiritual Support:

- **Faith Leaders:** Religious leaders, such as pastors, priests, and rabbis, can provide spiritual guidance and emotional support. They often offer a compassionate ear and can help individuals find meaning and solace during difficult times.
- **Faith Communities:** Participation in a faith community can provide a sense of belonging and collective support. Group activities, worship services, and community events foster connection and emotional well-being.

Building a Support System

1. Identifying Needs:

- **Assess Emotional Needs:** Determine the types of support needed, such as emotional validation, practical assistance, or encouragement. Identifying specific needs helps in seeking out appropriate support.

- **Recognize Gaps:** Identify areas where support may be lacking. This could involve areas of life where you feel isolated or unsupported and require additional resources.

2. Reaching Out:

- **Initiate Contact:** Reach out to family, friends, and acquaintances to build or strengthen connections. Initiating contact can be as simple as sending a message, making a phone call, or arranging a meeting.
- **Join Groups:** Participate in local or online groups that align with your interests or experiences. Joining groups provides opportunities to meet new people and expand your support network.

3. Building Trust:

- **Be Honest and Open:** Building trust involves being honest and open with others about your feelings and experiences.

Authentic communication fosters deeper connections and mutual understanding.

- **Respect Boundaries:** Respect the boundaries of others and ensure that interactions are mutually supportive. Healthy relationships are based on respect, trust, and reciprocity.

4. Offering Support:

- **Reciprocate Support:** Supportive relationships are reciprocal. Offer emotional and practical support to others in your network, creating a mutually beneficial dynamic.
- **Be Present:** Being present and attentive in interactions shows that you value and care about the other person. Active listening and empathy are key components of offering support.

5. Seeking Professional Help:

- **Therapeutic Relationships:** Establish a relationship with a mental health professional, such as a therapist or counselor. Regular sessions provide a safe space for exploring emotions and developing coping strategies.

- **Medical Support:** Consult healthcare providers for medical support and referrals to additional resources, such as support groups or specialized services.

6. Maintaining Relationships:

- **Regular Communication:** Stay in touch with supportive individuals through regular communication. This could involve phone calls, text messages, social media interactions, or face-to-face meetings.
- **Show Appreciation:** Express gratitude and appreciation for the support received. Acknowledging the efforts of others strengthens relationships and fosters a positive dynamic.

Strengthening Your Support System

1. Expanding Your Network:

- **Attend Events:** Participate in social events, community gatherings, and professional conferences to meet new people and expand your support network.
- **Volunteer:** Volunteering for community organizations or causes can introduce you to like-minded individuals and create opportunities for mutual support.

2. Nurturing Existing Relationships:

- **Quality Time:** Spend quality time with family and friends to nurture existing relationships. Shared activities and meaningful conversations deepen connections and enhance emotional support.
- **Conflict Resolution:** Address conflicts and misunderstandings promptly and constructively. Healthy conflict resolution maintains trust and strengthens relationships.

3. Building New Connections:

- **Be Open:** Be open to forming new connections and friendships. Approach new interactions with curiosity and a willingness to build supportive relationships.

- **Shared Interests:** Seek out individuals with shared interests or experiences. Common ground provides a foundation for building strong and supportive relationships.

4. Balancing Give and Take:

- **Equitable Support:** Ensure that support in relationships is balanced. Both giving and receiving support are essential for maintaining healthy and sustainable relationships.
- **Self-Care:** While offering support to others, prioritize self-care to maintain your own emotional well-being. Healthy boundaries ensure that you can provide support without becoming overwhelmed.

The Role of Friends and Family

Friends and family play a vital role in helping individuals manage negative emotions and achieve emotional well-being. This chapter explores how these relationships provide emotional support, practical assistance, and a sense of belonging, all of which are essential for mental health. By understanding the unique contributions of friends and family, individuals can better appreciate and cultivate these connections to foster a supportive and resilient environment.

Emotional Support

1. Listening and Empathy:
- **Active Listening:** Friends and family often serve as primary listeners when one needs to talk about their feelings. Active listening involves giving full attention, showing empathy, and responding thoughtfully, which helps individuals feel heard and validated.
- **Empathy:** Close relationships provide empathy, which involves understanding and sharing the feelings of others. This emotional

resonance can offer comfort and reassurance during difficult times.

2. Validation:

- **Affirmation of Feelings:** Family and friends can validate an individual's emotions by acknowledging their experiences without judgment. This affirmation helps individuals feel that their emotions are legitimate and understandable.
- **Reducing Self-Doubt:** Validation from loved ones can reduce self-doubt and encourage individuals to trust their feelings and perceptions, contributing to better emotional health.

3. Emotional Comfort:

- **Reassurance:** Friends and family provide reassurance during challenging times, reminding individuals that they are not alone and that they have support. This reassurance can be a powerful antidote to feelings of isolation and despair.

- **Emotional Availability:** Being emotionally available means being present and attentive when needed. Friends and family who are emotionally available can offer consistent support and comfort.

Practical Assistance

1. Day-to-Day Help:

- **Household Tasks:** Friends and family can assist with household chores, childcare, or other daily responsibilities, reducing the burden on individuals dealing with negative emotions. This practical help allows individuals to focus on their emotional recovery.
- **Logistical Support:** Loved ones can provide logistical support, such as transportation, running errands, or managing appointments, making it easier for individuals to navigate their daily lives during emotionally challenging periods.

2. Resource Sharing:

- **Information and Advice:** Friends and family often share valuable information and advice on coping strategies, mental health resources, and community services. This guidance can help individuals find effective ways to manage their emotions.
- **Networking:** Loved ones can leverage their networks to provide additional support, such as connecting individuals with helpful contacts, recommending therapists, or suggesting support groups.

3. Crisis Intervention:

- **Immediate Help:** In times of crisis, friends and family can provide immediate help, whether it's offering a safe place to stay, accompanying someone to seek medical attention, or simply being there to provide emotional support.
- **Long-Term Support:** Beyond immediate crises, loved ones can offer ongoing support through recovery and adjustment periods, ensuring that individuals do not have to face challenges alone.

Sense of Belonging

1. Social Connection:
- **Building Bonds:** Relationships with friends and family foster a sense of belonging and connection, which is crucial for emotional well-being. These bonds provide a supportive network that individuals can rely on during both good and bad times.
- **Community and Identity:** Being part of a family or friend group contributes to one's sense of identity and community. This connection can enhance self-esteem and provide a stable foundation for emotional health.

2. Shared Experiences:
- **Creating Memories:** Shared experiences with friends and family, such as holidays, celebrations, and everyday moments, create lasting memories and strengthen emotional bonds. These positive memories can serve as a source of comfort during tough times.

- **Traditions and Rituals:** Family traditions and rituals, such as holiday celebrations or weekly gatherings, provide a sense of continuity and stability. These practices reinforce the sense of belonging and emotional security.

3. Supportive Environment:

- **Safe Space:** Friends and family can create a safe and non-judgmental environment where individuals feel free to express their emotions and seek support. This safe space is essential for emotional exploration and healing.
- **Encouragement and Motivation:** Loved ones provide encouragement and motivation, helping individuals pursue their goals and maintain a positive outlook. This support fosters resilience and a sense of purpose.

Strengthening Relationships with Friends and Family

1. Effective Communication:
- **Open Dialogue:** Maintain open and honest communication with friends and family. Sharing thoughts and feelings openly fosters mutual understanding and strengthens relationships.
- **Active Listening:** Practice active listening by giving full attention to others and responding with empathy. This skill enhances the quality of interactions and builds trust.

2. Quality Time:
- **Regular Interaction:** Spend regular quality time with loved ones, whether through planned activities or casual gatherings. Consistent interaction reinforces emotional bonds and creates opportunities for support.

- **Meaningful Activities:** Engage in meaningful activities together, such as shared hobbies, volunteering, or exploring new interests. These experiences deepen connections and create positive memories.

3. Expressing Appreciation:
- **Gratitude:** Express gratitude for the support and presence of friends and family. Acknowledging their contributions strengthens relationships and fosters a positive dynamic.
- **Acts of Kindness:** Show appreciation through acts of kindness, such as thoughtful gestures, helping with tasks, or offering emotional support in return.

4. Setting Boundaries:
- **Healthy Boundaries:** Establish and respect healthy boundaries within relationships. Clear boundaries ensure that interactions remain supportive and respectful, preventing burnout and maintaining balance.

- **Self-Care:** Prioritize self-care to maintain emotional well-being. Taking care of oneself ensures that one can continue to provide and receive support effectively.

5. Conflict Resolution:

- **Addressing Issues:** Address conflicts and misunderstandings promptly and constructively. Healthy conflict resolution involves open communication, empathy, and a willingness to find mutually acceptable solutions.

- **Repairing Relationships:** After conflicts, take steps to repair and strengthen relationships. Apologize when necessary, offer forgiveness, and work together to rebuild trust.

Focusing on Strengths and Virtues

In the journey of Turning Negative Emotions into Positive Growth and fostering emotional well-being, focusing on strengths and virtues plays a pivotal role. This chapter explores the principles of positive psychology and how leveraging personal strengths and virtues can lead to transformative growth and resilience. By understanding and cultivating these positive attributes, individuals can enhance their capacity to navigate challenges and embrace a more fulfilling life.

Embracing Positive Psychology Principles

1. Definition of Positive Psychology:
- **Optimizing Human Potential:** Positive psychology is a branch of psychology that focuses on identifying and nurturing strengths and virtues in individuals, communities, and organizations. It emphasizes building resilience, fostering positive emotions, and promoting overall well-being.
- **Shift from Pathology:** Unlike traditional psychology, which primarily addresses

mental illness and dysfunction, positive psychology shifts the focus towards enhancing what is already going well in people's lives.

2. Core Principles:

- **Strengths and Virtues:** Positive psychology identifies character strengths and virtues as fundamental elements of human flourishing. These include qualities such as courage, wisdom, kindness, perseverance, and creativity.

- **Positive Emotions:** Cultivating positive emotions, such as joy, gratitude, hope, and love, enhances psychological resilience and overall life satisfaction.

- **Optimal Functioning:** The goal of positive psychology is to promote optimal functioning by leveraging strengths, fostering positive emotions, and nurturing meaningful connections.

Identifying Personal Strengths

1. Character Strengths Assessment:
- **Tools and Assessments:** Various assessments, such as the VIA Survey of Character Strengths, help individuals identify their unique strengths and virtues. These tools provide insights into core qualities that contribute to personal fulfillment and resilience.
- **Self-Reflection:** Reflective practices, journaling, and feedback from trusted individuals can also aid in recognizing strengths that may not be immediately apparent.

2. Types of Strengths:
- **Strengths of Wisdom and Knowledge:** These strengths include creativity, curiosity, open-mindedness, love of learning, and perspective-taking. They enable individuals to approach challenges with insight and adaptability.
- **Strengths of Courage:** Courage encompasses bravery, perseverance, honesty, and zest. These strengths empower

individuals to confront fears, take calculated risks, and persist in the face of adversity.

- **Strengths of Humanity:** Kindness, social intelligence, and empathy are examples of strengths that facilitate positive relationships and contribute to a sense of connectedness and belonging.

- **Strengths of Justice:** Fairness, leadership, teamwork, and citizenship promote a sense of responsibility towards others and foster a harmonious community.

- **Strengths of Temperance:** Self-regulation, humility, prudence, and forgiveness support balanced and mindful decision-making, contributing to emotional stability and well-being.

Cultivating Strengths for Resilience

1. Development and Application:

- **Strengths-Based Approach:** Adopting a strengths-based approach involves leveraging personal strengths to navigate challenges and achieve goals. This approach focuses on building on existing strengths rather than dwelling on weaknesses.

- **Skill Building:** Engaging in activities that align with personal strengths, such as hobbies, projects, or volunteer work, enhances competence and fosters a sense of accomplishment.
- **Continuous Growth:** Regular practice and refinement of strengths promote continuous growth and adaptation to changing circumstances.

2. Integration into Daily Life:

- **Mindful Application:** Practicing mindfulness and self-awareness facilitates the intentional use of strengths in daily interactions and decision-making.
- **Strengths in Relationships:** Recognizing and appreciating strengths in others strengthens interpersonal connections and promotes mutual support.
- **Goal Setting:** Setting goals that align with personal strengths enhances motivation and increases the likelihood of success.

Virtues and Their Impact

1. Understanding Virtues:

- **Definition and Importance:** Virtues are universally valued moral qualities that guide ethical behavior and promote a sense of integrity and purpose. Examples include honesty, compassion, fairness, and generosity.
- **Role in Well-Being:** Cultivating virtues contributes to a sense of moral character, enhances interpersonal relationships, and fosters a positive reputation within communities.

2. Integration with Strengths:

- **Synergy:** Virtues often complement and reinforce personal strengths, facilitating holistic growth and ethical decision-making.
- **Ethical Leadership:** Leaders who embody virtues inspire trust, promote fairness, and prioritize the well-being of others, creating inclusive and supportive environments.

Applying Positive Psychology Principles

1. Practical Strategies:
- **Gratitude Practices:** Regularly expressing gratitude cultivates positive emotions and enhances resilience in the face of adversity.
- **Savoring Positive Experiences:** Mindfully savoring enjoyable moments increases happiness and fosters a sense of fulfillment.
- **Acts of Kindness:** Engaging in acts of kindness towards others promotes altruism and strengthens social connections.

2. Personal Growth Journey:
- **Reflection and Adjustment:** Reflecting on experiences and adjusting strategies based on lessons learned promotes continuous personal growth and development.
- **Seeking Support:** Connecting with mentors, coaches, or peers who embody positive psychology principles provides encouragement and guidance in embracing strengths and virtues.

Creating a Personal Growth Plan

Creating a personal growth plan is essential for individuals seeking to maximize their potential, achieve goals, and foster overall well-being. This chapter explores the process of developing a personalized roadmap for growth, emphasizing self-reflection, goal setting, and actionable steps to cultivate strengths, manage emotions, and enhance life satisfaction.

Importance of a Personal Growth Plan

1. Clarity and Direction:

Vision Setting: A personal growth plan provides clarity by defining long-term aspirations and goals. It helps individuals articulate their vision for personal development and establish a clear direction for their journey.

Focus and Prioritization: By outlining priorities and objectives, a growth plan enables individuals to focus their time and energy on activities that align with their values and aspirations.

2. Motivation and Accountability:

Goal Setting: Setting specific, measurable, achievable, relevant, and time-bound (SMART) goals within the growth plan enhances motivation and commitment to personal growth. It provides benchmarks for progress and achievement.

Accountability: The structured nature of a growth plan encourages individuals to hold themselves accountable for their actions and progress towards goals. Regular review and reflection reinforce accountability.

Steps to Create a Personal Growth Plan

1. Self-Assessment and Reflection:

- **Identify Strengths and Areas for Improvement:** Conduct a thorough self-assessment to identify personal strengths, virtues, skills, and areas where improvement is desired. Reflect on past experiences, achievements, challenges, and lessons learned.

- **Values Clarification:** Clarify personal values and principles that guide decision-making and shape goals. Aligning goals with values enhances motivation and ensures consistency with personal beliefs.

2. Goal Setting:

- **SMART Goals:** Develop SMART goals that are specific, measurable, achievable, relevant, and time-bound. Break down long-term objectives into smaller, actionable steps to facilitate progress and momentum.
- **Short-term and Long-term Goals:** Define short-term goals to achieve within weeks or months, as well as long-term goals that span one to five years. Balance immediate milestones with aspirational objectives for comprehensive growth.

3. Action Planning:

- **Identify Action Steps:** Outline specific action steps required to achieve each goal.

Determine resources, skills, and support needed to implement action plans effectively.

- **Timeline and Deadlines:** Establish a timeline with deadlines for completing action steps and achieving milestones. Regularly review progress and adjust timelines as necessary to maintain momentum.

4. Skill Development and Learning:

- **Continuous Learning:** Identify opportunities for skill development, knowledge acquisition, and personal growth. Engage in formal education, workshops, seminars, online courses, or self-study to expand competencies and capabilities.
- **Skill Application:** Apply newly acquired skills and knowledge in practical settings to reinforce learning and build proficiency. Seek feedback and mentorship to enhance skill development.

Integrating Emotional Management Strategies

1. Emotional Awareness:

- **Self-Reflection:** Cultivate self-awareness by reflecting on emotions, triggers, and patterns of response in various situations. Recognize strengths in emotional regulation and areas requiring improvement.
- **Mindfulness Practices:** Incorporate mindfulness techniques, such as meditation, deep breathing exercises, or mindful journaling, to enhance emotional awareness and reduce stress.

2. Emotion Regulation Techniques:

- **Stress Management:** Develop effective stress management strategies, such as time management, relaxation techniques, or physical exercise, to mitigate the impact of stressors on emotional well-being.

- **Coping Mechanisms:** Identify healthy coping mechanisms, such as creative outlets, social support, or hobbies, to manage negative emotions and maintain resilience during challenging times.

Evaluating Progress and Adjusting Strategies

1. Regular Review and Reflection:
- **Assess Progress:** Periodically evaluate progress towards goals and milestones outlined in the growth plan. Celebrate achievements and acknowledge areas for improvement.
- **Feedback Mechanisms:** Seek feedback from mentors, peers, or trusted advisors to gain insights and perspectives on personal growth efforts. Use feedback to refine goals and action plans.

2. Adaptability and Flexibility:
- **Adjustment of Plans:** Remain adaptable and flexible in response to changing circumstances, opportunities, or setbacks.

Modify goals, action steps, or timelines as needed to align with evolving priorities and aspirations.

- **Resilience Building:** Cultivate resilience by learning from setbacks, leveraging strengths, and maintaining a positive outlook on personal growth journey.

Personal Growth Plan Example

1. Long-term Goal:

- **Goal:** Attain proficiency in leadership skills to advance to a management role within five years.
- **SMART Objective:** Complete a leadership development program within two years to acquire necessary skills and competencies.
- **Action Steps:** Enroll in leadership courses, participate in leadership workshops, seek mentorship from experienced leaders, and apply new skills in current role.

2. Short-term Goal:

- **Goal:** Improve public speaking skills to confidently deliver presentations within six months.
- **SMART Objective:** Attend public speaking classes and practice delivering speeches at local community events.
- **Action Steps:** Schedule regular practice sessions, join Toastmasters International for feedback and support, and record and review presentations for self-assessment.

CONCLUSION

Transforming Negativity into Positive Growth

In "Turning Negative Emotions into Positive Growth: Transforming Negativity into Positive Growth, Lasting Resilience, and Lifelong Emotional Well-Being," we embarked on a transformative journey to explore strategies and insights aimed at fostering emotional resilience and well-being. Throughout this book, we delved into various topics and approaches that empower individuals to navigate and transcend negative emotions effectively.

Embracing Emotional Awareness and Understanding

We began by acknowledging the significance of emotional awareness and understanding. Recognizing and identifying triggers, both past and present, allows us to gain insights into our emotional responses. By embracing mindfulness and self-reflection, we cultivate the ability to manage and regulate our emotions proactively.

Leveraging Strengths and Virtues

Central to our journey was the exploration of positive psychology principles. By focusing on strengths and virtues, individuals harness their innate capabilities to thrive amidst challenges. We identified personal strengths through assessments and self-reflection, integrating them into daily life to foster resilience and personal growth.

Strategies for Emotional Management

Effective emotional management strategies were pivotal in our exploration. From reframing negative thoughts to engaging in healthy expression and journaling, these techniques empower individuals to navigate emotional landscapes with clarity and purpose. Mindfulness practices and the power of journaling emerged as transformative tools in cultivating self-awareness and emotional well-being.

Building a Personal Growth Plan

Creating a personalized growth plan emerged as a cornerstone of our journey towards emotional resilience. By setting SMART goals, identifying action steps, and integrating emotional management strategies, individuals can progress towards their aspirations with intentionality and accountability. Continuous learning, skill development, and adaptability are key components in this ongoing journey of self-improvement.

Strengthening Relationships and Seeking Support

Recognizing the interconnectedness between emotional well-being and relationships, we explored the role of friends, family, and professional support systems. Building and maintaining supportive relationships foster empathy, communication, and a sense of belonging, enhancing overall emotional health.

The Power of Positive Psychology

Throughout our exploration, positive psychology illuminated pathways towards lasting emotional well-being. Cultivating gratitude, savoring positive experiences, and engaging in acts of kindness contribute to a positive mindset and resilience in the face of adversity. By embracing optimism and focusing on what is within our control, individuals can cultivate a sense of agency and empowerment in their lives.

Embracing the Journey Towards Emotional Well-Being

As we conclude our journey, it becomes clear that Turning Negative Emotions into Positive Growth is not merely about avoidance or suppression but rather about transformation and growth. By integrating these strategies and insights into daily practices, individuals can embark on a path towards lasting resilience, personal fulfillment, and lifelong emotional well-being.

Let us continue to embrace the challenges and opportunities that come with managing emotions, knowing that each experience is an opportunity for growth and self-discovery. May this journey empower you to navigate life's complexities with courage, compassion, and a deep-seated belief in your inherent strength and resilience.

www.ingramcontent.com/pod-product-compliance
Lightning Source LLC
Chambersburg PA
CBHW070822250726
48662CB00003B/1051